Walk-Ons and Bit-Parts

WALK-ONS AND BIT-PARTS

Sara Lee Stadelman

For Ruth Bluger,
Best wishes,
Sara Lee Stadelman

Penumbra Press

This is a first edition published by Penumbra Press. Printed and bound in Canada.

Cover design: Rob Fillion
Cover photo: Sara Lee Stadelman in rehearsal for *The New Canticle*, M.W.C. archive
Copy editing: Douglas Campbell
Printed in Canada by Coach House Printing
Published by Penumbra Press

Canadian Cataloguing in Publication Data

Stadelman, Sara Lee, 1917-
Walk-ons and bit-parts

ISBN 1-894131-09-6

Stadelman, Sara Lee, 1917- 2. Actors—Canada—Biography.
3. Theater—Canada—Biography. I. Title.

PN2308.S72A3 2000 792'028'092 C00-901371-7

The publisher gratefully acknowledges the Canada Council for the Arts for supporting Penumbra Press's publishing programme.

The author and publisher wish to thank Mr Tappan Wilder for permission to cite from letters by Isabel Wilder and Thornton Wilder.

It is with gratitude and wonder that I treasure those saints and sinners whose names are too numerous to list.

CONTENTS

PUBLISHER'S FOREWORD

My attraction to Sara Lee Stadelman's story began in part with the manuscript's inspired covering letter claiming that "A good part of the pleasure in reading Ms Stadelman's memoir is that she confines her sense of sequence to her theme (the constant tension between art and faith) rather than the chronology of her life." These words struck me as anticipating the type of memoir I am eager to read and publish — one in which the author's take on personal circumstances goes beyond the mundane realities of who, what, where, etc., and reaches into the effervescent mélange of an incisive imagination and a seductive aesthetic.

In that regard, this memoir reads sometimes like fiction, sometimes like poetry, and sometimes like fantasy. Readers who have difficulty distinguishing between art and reality may find this attribute disconcerting. Yet it is a story that is as fine a representation of life-writing as I have read.

Perhaps it is fascination with the performing arts that tweaks our attention in her story; maybe it is the intensity of the experiences themselves, regardless of whether or not the theatre is a backdrop; or perhaps it is an acknowledged but hidden commitment of transformation. Whatever it is, the reader is rewarded with a story of rapid vibrancy.

— John Flood, Publisher

Jesus in the Window

"DR. B, I'M FALLING FROM SIDE TO SIDE, losing my balance like an old woman."

"Well-l-l ... " Quietly he lingered on those liquid ells ...

"Yes." I finished for him, to cover his embarrassment. "Yes," I repeated, "I am an old woman."

But that's not all of it. I can still do a *grand plié* without any difficulty, without quivering. Dr. C and Dr. D were both impressed.

"You're spectacular for a woman of eighty."

Years of practice. But try me on a slow walk along any city street, ten yards and I'm panting: it's the heat, it's not enough sleep, it's anxiety.

It was those who loved me best stamped 80 on my forehead, against my will, damn it! I've never thought of myself as *eighty*. Seventy, maybe, and of course I admitted to sixty-five when I garnered those needed perks. But eighty!

They'd planned a surprise party but their plans fell through, thank God. I could take all those aborted invitations and press them like dried flowers in memory's album. Camellias and dandelions.

* * * * *

My forty-eight-year-old daughter Cate joyously bursts into the room. She's been out in the still-frozen park gathering what's left of last summer's yield. It's been a long, cold winter.

"They're all I could find," she says, and begins to arrange them in a tall blue hand-blown glass that's part of a diminishing set we've treasured over the years.

I touch the grey velvet milkweed pods gently, run my fingers over the dried Queen Anne's lace, the reeds, the cattails.

"My farewell present!" she beams, holds me close. And is gone.

Where *does* childhood go? Under my skin. In my bones.

* * * * *

Irene, my little Catholic friend — I can't think Irene without thinking Catholic — lived down the block with her mother and father, Mr. and Mrs. Wing, and three grown-up sisters, Florence, Elsie, and Ruth. They wore high heels and only looked our way if my mother said hello or good morning. We weren't Catholics. There was an older brother, William, too. He was very thin and tired-looking and worked far away from Brooklyn in the State of Massachusetts. (I learned to spell that in third grade.) Irene told me her big brother found a "bride" there. She said, too, "I can write 'Mass.' on an envelope if I send him a letter because there are lots of Catholics in Massachusetts." Anyway, William came home to Brooklyn without his "bride" and no one ever talked about him again because hecommittedsuicide. *Don't say it*; they're *Catholic*!

Our world was the length of our long street. East Seventh was a friendly one in its way. Catholic, Protestant, and three Jewish families exchanged greetings, tidbits of news, and non-threatening gossip. Everyone joined in the annual block parties and Fourth of July fireworks celebrations. The boys played baseball, the girls, except for the very young, remained aloof, warned by their parents to be "good" and not forget that one day you'll be someone's *bride*. From time to time neighbours visited a home where a person had died — in those days the dead were waked at home — but families cocooned in worlds of their own kept our block fairly quiet. It was important "not to let anyone know your business."

Irene looked like my favourite childhood comic strip, "Ella Cinders," whose name was, of course, an anagram for "Cinderella." Both Irene and Ella had black bobbed hair and long bangs; their faces were peppered with freckles, which I envied so much that I dotted my face with brown crayon until my mother made me scrub them off. "The neighbours will think you have measles, or chicken pox!"

Before we went to our different schools, Irene and I had "adventures." On my front stoop we ate peaches in the summertime, sucked the pits dry and tried to scrape them hollow on the cement to make rings for our pinky fingers. If they didn't fit — and they never did — I'd say damn! and one day I said it so loud the mailman heard me. He said he was going to tell my mother; that made me mad and so together Irene and I hid under the hydrangea bush and yelled, damn! damn! damn! The mailman did tell on us, and my dad had to wash my mouth with soap. My mother said she was too aggravated to do it, but I saw her mouth twist trying to smother a laugh.

She told me that the mailman was a nice gentleman and we gave him a present every Christmas. I guess my grandfather didn't see her do that because he wouldn't let us have a Christmas tree like the goyim and I had to go to Irene's to see the beautiful candles lit for Jesus' birthday. Damn, damn, damn. Was the mailman Catholic?

On Irene's front stoop, we would check to see if her mother was using the rocking chair. We were allowed up on their porch to take turns rocking until Mrs. Wing came out to pray her rosary, then we had to sit on the steps and BE STILL.

It could take a long time.

Once, when Mrs. Wing stopped rocking and praying long enough to go inside to "mind the bread rising," we didn't take our turns rocking. Instead, Irene whisked me to the corner at the far end of the street where there was a rock pit behind the Lutheran church.

I whisper, "You're not supposed to come here!"

"Don't tell," she says.

We're lucky nobody's around. Irene is excited. "Let's go down."

I look. It's deep enough to hold Paul Bunyan and his Blue Ox!

We sit on the rim of the rock pit and slide as far as our bottoms will take us, then we use our hands and feet to go from boulder to boulder, but we keep slipping and the rocks start tumbling, faster and faster. When they stop, we're in the middle of a huge circle and all we can see is the church's slanted roof. It's scary. We begin to climb back up, but every time we grab one rock, a few more roll down. We crawl from one side to another, our hands and knees bleeding. We keep reaching and letting go. Irene pulls my shoe, I pull her skirt. I'm crying, help! help! help! Irene's crying, Jesusmaryandjoseph! We find a perch, then a foothold, and at last we get to the top.

We're both sobbing. Irene gulps, "Jesus is punishing me; I disobeyed my mother. And you!" She points at me, "You tore my dress!" She runs home.

I point to the bottom of the rock pile. "And you!" I scream, "You lost my shoe!" I limp back home. My dress is OK, but I've wet my pants.

* * * * *

That Lutheran church on the corner — it must have had a name — held a special fascination for us: Irene because it was forbidden territory for a Catholic, and me because its stained-glass window fronted our street; its ledge was just low enough for me to sit on and look at a serious Jesus talking to little children. One was sitting on His lap. You could see Jesus was telling a very good story, all the children were listening to Him. So was I. In fact, I was the one sitting on His lap. This was an especially nice way to spend time on days when Irene couldn't play with me because she had to go to the doctor for her "kidneytrouble." That vibrant window made the King James Bible my sister and I read, real. Every day we read it with Mary Baker Eddy's *Science and Health with a Key to the Scriptures*. Jesus in the window wasn't telling me what to do like all the grownups did. He was kind; he'd already told grownups to leave us kids alone, shooed them away when they said we'd be too much trouble. He said: Let Them Come Unto Me.

And there we were, just Jesus and me! My secret friend.

I wanted to see the inside of this church that had such a friendly Jesus in its window. Mr. Bourquist, the minister, lived across the street from us, but of course he never invited us to attend his services — not that that would stop Catholic Irene.

(The good Reverend smiled our way when he walked to his church on the corner. If my grandfather saw him he'd nod his yarmulked head as if returning the greeting, murmur a Yiddish curse sotto voce, go to the curb, wait until he saw the back of the clerical collar, and then jettison a stream of pee in the direction of such goyim. But remember: when my grandfather was little like me he had to run away from his Russian village in terror. The last thing he saw was Christian Cossacks burning it — and actually crucifying his parents).

One day Irene had news: there was going to be a wedding in Mr. Bourquist's church! The "bride" was the daughter of Mr. and Mrs. Hellmann, the MAYONNAISE people. It was going to be "splendid," since we all ate mayonnaise every day — everyone in the whole world ate mayonnaise — and the Hellmanns would be rich. There'd be lots of bridesmaids and flowers and beautiful dresses.

"We can just look and watch the big cars and the wedding party," Irene says. "When everyone's in the church, we can sneak in and see them GET MARRIED!" She pulls me into the church and we stay crouched until the organ's final crashing chords.

When the people leave the church a surprised usher gives us each a handful of rice and we run outside to toss it at a cloud of white tulle Irene says is The Bride!

It was fun, but there was something I couldn't understand: the Jesus in the window didn't seem to come inside the church.

Every Saturday I follow Irene to her church, St. Rose of Lima, where she goes to Confession. (I know she has to tell about going into the Lutheran church.) I sit alone in the quiet dark waiting for her. I secretly finger the amber beads I'd snuck from my mother's jewellery box, because Irene had taught me the first half of the rosary.

I hear whispers from the curtained confessionals; they're gentle whispers, not the fierce ones I try to overhear at home, not the forbidden secrets about my crippled sister who everybody can see is crippled but nobody will talk about — not even use the word cripple — and I have to sleep next to her and look after her when she has her seizures even though she's ten years older than me. I wait, my eyes glued to the red sanctuary lamp, expecting that angels will come, or visions. Irene promised me they did. Sometimes.

When Irene finishes her Confession she walks real fast away from me to the front pew; she kneels with her head down to pray some beads.

Once she stayed so long her beads didn't rattle and I got scared. I tiptoed up the aisle to see if she was alright. I stopped when I saw what she was looking at. Behind the soft sanctuary lamp, in the middle of the dark altar, was a huge cross with Jesus on it. He was in pain, I could tell. There was blood on His open hands, on His side, on His feet. He didn't move. He was alone.

When Irene got up we walked back to East Seventh Street not saying much, so I thought about the Jesus who hurt, the Jesus I loved at St. Rose of Lima. I thought about the Jesus I loved in the window. I thought, If Jesus ever has "a bride," I want it to be me.

* * * * *

Now if I could find, create, some characters to be decoded by those who wouldn't be put off by my turbulent feelings, but like ancient Jews who revere God's name so much that they don't speak it aloud, I might be able to describe my attachment to Christ, my gripping love so stormy as not to be spoken, that drags me down, pulls me through, lifts me up. No sentimental wintered slush this, but a rush of seasons born of waiting.

* * * * *

Irene went to Catholic school and I to P.S. 179; the street divided silently. Where is she now? Did she live to be eighty, too, despite her "kidneytrouble"? Does she know how beguiled I was when I accompanied her to Saturday confession, silently saying the first half of that rosary she'd taught me when we'd played school? (I didn't learn the second half until thirty years later, when my older brother, also a convert to the Catholic church, taught me.)

I am younger now than I've ever been. The park's hard-pressed paths, where my daughter Cate gathered last year's wild flowers, stun me with the promise of sweet surprises.

Isa

THE BELL RANG ONE DAY in our classroom. Its two-ring signal meant that the principal had a message and needed a messenger. The pupil who could sit tallest and had been best-behaved that morning would be given the privilege. No competition there. I was the smallest, but I always sat and stood tallest.

In the principal's office I was literally handed a pretty girl my own age. She was introduced: Toussia Kremer. I was told to deliver her to my teacher, a new member for our class. To my surprise the teacher moved another pupil and seated the new girl next to me.

She was Russian, a foreign-born exotic. She spoke English, German, and French, too, besides Russian. Her name was pronounced *Tooshya*, so I called her Teek in order to cover my embarrassment when others mockingly called her *Tushy*. I added the K as an abbreviation for her family name, Kremer.

Teek accepted me as a friend and I eagerly followed her home where she introduced me to my first taste of blini, peroshki, caviar — and to her mother, Isa. In Isa I touched another world, a world to which I knew instantly I belonged. Theatre. For Isa was in the theatre — a live performer! She sang folk songs in languages that until then I'd only heard on scratchy Victrola records.

Teek's house was about a mile from mine geographically, but planets away actually. It became my gateway to Isa and Isa became my escape to beauty from deformity, from my crippled sister, to whom I was tethered albatross-like day and night. My home was a middle-class maze of quarrels and confusion where the only sweet sounds were those I imagined; hers a rambling Bohemian affair, arranged for only one child, two old grandparents, and a special area set aside for the piano, where Isa practised alongside music albums piled every which way.

Other rooms were of no interest to me except for Isa's. It was large, light, crammed with closets and costumes and, best of all, her makeup table. It wasn't often that I was permitted to watch her apply delicious-smelling paints, when she returned from concert tours and readied herself for a New York engagement. I wonder now whether I had the privilege — for that's what I considered it to be — more than once or twice.

Isa at her dressing table with a lighted match, warming a tiny pan of black mascara, globules of which tipped each eyelash and highlighted the shining green shadow on her lids; Isa whose wide mouth became a vibrant gash of red; Isa whose Tatar cheekbones were painted high to ensure a mask so striking, so individual that no one could mistake her for any other woman. To me she was unique, she was theatre, a magnet, a world of secret promise. Isa Kremer was an empire in which I wanted citizenship.

Her hair, jet black, parted in the centre, drawn back fiercely in a chignon, proclaimed Pavlova; her earrings, her jewelled fingers tapping secret codes, flashing emeralds, diamonds, sapphires stolen cunningly in flight to exile. When Isa had at last secured her makeup, patting the greased colours with a feathery pink puff, I could tell she — I — was ready to face the world.

As I grew into adolescence, I became aware of her body, and then only because I saw the identical pattern fitted onto her daughter: short-necked, high-breasted, hipless, long-legged for such squat women. But Isa's shawls, trailing skirts, and voluminous sleeves craftily covered multitudes of roundnesses. No sagging was to be observed, nothing but energy, as she prepared herself to receive Russian friends for lengthy dinners that began while it was still light and went on long after I had to go home.

Teek and I were welcomed to that round table of celebrities, where expansive Chaliapin's basso profundo laughter mocked ambitious Sol Hurok, already grasping for worldwide recognition as *the* impresario.

It was in Isa's dining room that everything Russian came alive. The tiny grandparents would scuttle from the kitchen bearing fruit soup or succulent Chicken Kiev. Confined to backstage, they would disappear, muttering to themselves.

Who made all that? Not Isa. It must have been hired help in the kitchen supervised by the unacknowledged grandparents.

Who were the other men surrounding Isa? For there were no other women at that groaning board. Actors? Singers? Agents? They were refugees from the Russian Revolution, unpolitical, fleeing both Whites and Reds. They were artists grasping for a foothold in "the land of opportunity" to continue their professions.

What I saw, what I heard, was laughter, a joy I'd never before known. What difference did it make to me that Russian, French, and broken English bounced around the noisy table like ricocheting projectiles — jokes, arguments, opinions? Did they hear each other? Who cared? This was life! In my home there was no time for me to be heard, but for some reason these strange people liked me! Yes. These adults asked *me* questions, listened to my answers. One giant of a man, with a voice deeper than any I'd ever heard, was delighted to put me on his knee.

"*Shtota koi*, little Sara, *shtohochesh*?"

What did I want to be? I'd known that since I was three. And here in this place, with these thrilling performers, what else could I want but to be as glamorous as Isa, as talented and famous and adored?

"Oh, please," I declared breathlessly, "*pujalasta* — ACTRISA!"

"Bravo, little one!" He rose majestically, lifted me to the floor, and called for a toast. Everyone stood with glasses raised. Bravos! Cheers! They drank deeply, vodka to my ginger ale, and one by one smashed their glasses against the unused fireplace — in my honour! And this gentle giant, whom Isa told me to call Chaliapin, beamed at me, "*Zemechachina!*"

And where was Teek? Smiling, mumbling sotto voce in any of the four languages at her command, with an adult toss of her beautiful auburn hair, what was she really saying? I think now that I cared little about Teek, her feelings, her situation. She was so grown-up, always studying, reading books by writers I didn't know but made sure to read and then didn't understand. Within a couple of years she'd introduced me to bookshelves of Oscar Wilde, Omar Khayyam, Anatole France, Edna St. Vincent Millay, and to a panoply of characters that my now adolescent heart fell in love with: Heloise and Abelard, Salome (with illustrations by Aubrey Beardsley — quite naughty!).

At Isa's table there was one quiet man, only occasionally, gently, offering a phrase, a word, a comment. He was Isa's manager. And he lived in the same house. He was Greek. He was frequently out of town booking tours, so far out of town that he died in South America while booking Isa's Farewell Grand Tour. I knew there was a mystery there, a mystery of love between Isa and this man, but I was a child and could not penetrate it. Finally a ninth-grader, another new friend, a very sophisticated German girl, told me that George — ah! that was his name! — was more than Isa's manager. Isa was George's mistress. His what?

"Isa and George are not married but they do things to each other."

It took me time to absorb that. Time to refocus on *my* picture, my fantasy of Isa bountifully distributing her largesse to *me*.

Isa was the one who reserved an opera box for Teek and me whenever we went to the theatre, and it was there that I first saw "live" dancers. An opera box! Teek and I were twelve or thirteen by now and sufficiently conscious of our appearance to preen for special occasions. An opera box was such an occasion! But would people stare up at us? At me? On buses and subways, in movie theatres and restaurants, terrible moans and kicking at everything would signal the start of my sister's epileptic fit, and I felt everyone staring at me. I hated it. Now, at the theatre, I'd wait for the house lights to go down before I took my place; then the stage, bright with the *real* world, protected me.

From opera boxes I saw Mary Wigman before she returned to the nascent Nazi Germany; the politically prophetic Joos

Ballet, which satirized the League of Nations; and, most exciting of all, Isadora Duncan's youthful troupe of adoptees from the Soviet Union.

Wigman captivated me with her powerful percussive movements. I had free passage backstage with Isa's daughter. For the first and only time in my life I asked for an autograph. In awe, I watched Wigman sign my program. I noted her dyed red hair disconcertingly black at the roots, her creped aging skin raked with sweat. She was real, too. But not glamorous. Not like Isa.

The Duncan dancers, young, fresh, romantic, dashed across the stage, their red banners flying to the ecstatic strains of the Internationale. Of course! This was Russian! This was the faith with which I now could identify. When at last I saw Isa Kremer herself in performance, it was at *The Chauve Souris*. That was where New Yorkers caught the star turns of world-renowned Russian singers, dancers, jugglers. Their monologues and dramatic excerpts were "not to be missed!"

Isa's magical interpretation of folk songs came as no surprise. She *became* French, German, Italian. The audience was enraptured with every subtle nuance of character. For me none of it was unexpected. She was magic because I needed magic. *They* might see an actress, applaud a star; I knew her, recognized all of her. She was *me* fully dimensioned, encapsulating my dreams, my wishes. I applauded myself. I loved Isa for pointing the way, the direction to my future. I'd follow the Russians from samovar to stardom; it was all one to me.

When Isa was absent I made do with the huge posters of her that decorated every wall of every room in her shambling Brooklyn house. I heard in that absence the worn piano I'd listened to as I sat still while Isa practised singing scales. I haunted the glass-clinking dining room, where the smells of dillweed and bay leaf wafted in from the kitchen and the excitement around the table mingled with my images of music, dancing, red banners, Russia — the romance of my first hint of a world community especially for artists. Isa and Russia struck the match that ignited my childhood and adolescence.

There was a rare outing when Isa took Teek and me to the Roerich Museum. It was the only time the three of us were ever alone together. The museum was in the distant upper suburbs of New York City. We were chauffeured in a rented car. I remember our conversation centred on Shakespeare's Seven Ages of Man. I embarked upon an imagined painting, describing how I'd compose it. Isa listened, enjoying the details of my fantasy. Teek quietly tolerated our conversation.

When we arrived at the museum, Isa was welcomed by Nicholas Konstantinovich Roerich himself. Teek and I were left to admire the stark, stern icons glaring at the other Russian artifacts. I had to turn my back on them to admire the hand-embroidered costumes of peasants and princesses, complex and exotic, most of which are now entirely forgotten. Not so Isa's interest in me and my ideas.

Teek and I separated as we shaped into adolescence. It couldn't work. She was a better student, a mature teenager. She introduced me to one of her American Russian boyfriends. He was short, dark, and handsome, and my first embarrassing crush. He was a few years older and determined to be an actor. He sent me an elaborate Valentine, which I treasured secretly and never answered. I met him many years later when I studied at The Neighborhood Playhouse and found him working as assistant to Sanford Meisner. We had no further contact, but I remember how I resented hearing he'd married a Russian girl. A dancer? Actress? I saw her once or twice and pronounced her plain!

Teek went to Barnard, I to New College, an experimental division of Teacher's College, Columbia University. With my teenage marriage to a fellow student, a brilliant Marxist intellectual, Russia and the Russians took on a completely different colour. Avidly, my husband drew me into political activism. My interest in theatre tilted left, not only because of Duncan's dancers' red banners, but also performers like

Tamiris, whose Socialist Realist choreography now appeared in the WPA repertoire. At my young husband's urging I studied dance in Greenwich Village with Franziska Boaz, daughter of anthropologist Franz Boaz. She taught with an array of percussion that would be the envy of any philharmonic orchestra, and her beat became steadily more intense as her eyes and occasionally her hands fondled the only other woman in the class besides myself.

Percussion was also the basic accompaniment in Hanya Holm's classes. Her beat was Germanic, her attitude toward the less-experienced contemptuous. I came under her influence again at Bennington School of the Dance, where her rehearsals were tortured algebraic equations, shouted in anger. Between jobs, *jetés*, and late-night removals from apartments where rent was overdue, I found time to teach avid deprived students in the ghetto at Grand Street Settlement House. There I developed my first real taste for choreography.

All this was happening in the swirling late thirties, when artists were swimming in and against social currents. But who to swim with? I wanted to explore movement's depth. I transferred from Hanya Holm's approach to Martha Graham's. I couldn't afford to study with her, but I could scrape up enough to study and perform with her former dancer, Marie Marchowsky. In Marie's studio the rewarding struggle with Martha's technique, from its early primitive days to its then current evolution, was highlighted by arguments of religious intensity among us over Zionism versus Communism that left me far removed from my Christian orientation. Then, influenced by my scholarly husband and his friends, my faith shifted to Stalin's Utopia.

Yet I surreptitiously hid my Bible. I couldn't throw it out.

And Isa receded.

It was after a hiatus of fifteen years that I saw one of her last performances in a run-down downtown New York theatre.

I'd left Broadway, moved from New York and my first marriage, gone to Las Vegas and settled hopefully into a second. Fearful of the accelerating red-baiting, I'd had my private book-burning to avoid any hint that I'd once married a Marxist.

On one of my flying visits back east, my mother surprised me by saying she'd seen an announcement in the *New York Times* of Isa Kremer's "final appearance" before returning to Venezuela. I'd never known that Isa had left the States or that she was still performing.

I invited my mother to a matinee. We had no trouble getting tickets. There were no reserved seats, only folding chairs in this Second Avenue Theater that had been famous as the home of Yiddish theatre.

The audience was noisy, mostly middle-aged women who volubly hushed each other when Isa appeared onstage. Was there a curtain, or had it disappeared with my adolescence?

That day Isa sang only Yiddish songs, which my mother barely understood and I not at all. Yet Isa's interpretation, her eloquent gestures, and her mobile features brought each character and situation in her repertoire alive. She knew every trick to compensate when her voice now quivered in its upper register. Her energy and charm remained as electric as when I'd seen her in *The Chauve Souris* those years ago. That's why, I guess, there was no curtain between us — not until I went backstage to say thank you.

The most unexpected thing happened. She pulled me aside and in her deep unmistakable voice whispered, "Sara, I am like you now."

I looked at her. "Like me?" I held her wrinkled hands tightly in my firm ones. I wondered if she was hallucinating, wishing for her vanished youth, her once-blooming career …

"Like me?"

She winked one mascared lid, still dotted with black wax although waxed lashes had long gone out of fashion.

She repeated, "Like you, Sara. Communist!"

Nonplussed, I undid our hands, smiled, hugged, said goodbye.

Martha

It's the first time I've seen Martha Graham offstage, without costume: daunting, elegant, and, for me, breathtaking. Not a black hair is out of place on that slick skull, her scarlet lips draw back to reveal a surprisingly high-pitched voice and a threatening smile. *Her* face is restrained, the indomitable sharp-boned jaw masks her secret world, magical, fierce, enchanting. Violent. Oh, God, this is theatre! I am completely bowled over.

Is she speaking to me? I've heard almost nothing of what she's been saying but answer her few questions in stage-struck awe. My inner eye sees Martha dancing her wrenching "Lamentation," her taut body stretching within a grey wool cocoon.

"Yes," she says, "if you work hard there is a place for you here."

* * * * *

Her voice entices me to new and dangerous shores.

She seems to be sitting gravely still, facing me. But I see her left leg sweeping in a *grand battement* that almost grazes her ear. Ah! Copland's *Appalachian Spring*!

No, she sits here, smiling. Then as she says goodbye she shakes my hand. "Nice dry firm hand," she compliments me, and I know my audition is a success. I've won a scholarship to the Neighborhood Playhouse School of the Theater!

It was the Depression. Martha needed the financial and social support of the school. She also needed its affluent backers, the Lewisohns, the Rothschilds, the Morgenthaus.

But Martha hated to teach. She especially hated those for whom dance was of secondary importance. She supposed me to be committed. She'd given me her approbation and a scholarship as an eager dancer. She didn't know about my growing ambition to study acting at The Playhouse, where Sanford Meisner was reputed to be New York's master acting teacher.

Martha and Sandy conducted a quiet rivalry at The Playhouse. She was the celebrity, taking off her mask only in the act of creating. He was the actor, unmasking every creation. Like Graham, he urged us to leave the intellect behind and delve into our guts. But there the similarity ended. Made privy to our limitations and potential, Sandy nurtured each student. Martha was committed only to her own work. Students were of consequence to her only if they had promise for her performing company.

We are warming up at the barre, the men limbering as seriously as the women.

Martha demands neatness, orderly dress. We are all in the customary leotards and tights, except for Anna who can only afford a leotard and works with bare legs. Martha, as always, teaches in street clothes, chic, groomed for appointments from which we are keeping her: John Martin the critic, or Halston the couturier, or perhaps Isamu Noguchi the set designer.

Not a sound but for an occasional intake of a deep breath or strained exhalation as the class tries to achieve Martha's specific angry instruction.

"Lift the working leg bent at the knee. Directly in front. Hip level. And keep your standing leg straight! Now open the thigh to the side. Keep your working knee bent!"

The orders come with the speed and precision of bullets. Openthethighcompletely. Bendyourknee. AT PELVIS LEVEL! OPEN! Lift, open, reach. Lean forward. EXtend!

"ANNA," her voice ascends, "I said open the pelvis, OPEN. *OPEN!* Not like that. You are not *open*." Martha shrieks, "WHAT ARE YOU DOING? Watch *her*!" She points to me.

There is a sob. Anna says, "I'm trying."

"YOU ARE NOT TRYING. You are stupid!"

I turn from the barre to help Anna but before I can see what is happening there is a rush of clicking heels. Martha is racing toward us, the wooden clothes hanger that she has hurriedly picked up to beat out the rhythm for her favourite technical sequence clenched in her hand. A resounding crack of wood against bare flesh, an animal whine. Martha has struck the inside of Anna's thigh.

Martha turns on her heel, walks to the front of the room, smoothly, effortlessly as only she can walk, smiles bewitchingly and continues directing the stunned class.

I can still see the red splash on Anna's tender very white skin. She is a gentle girl, earnest, untalented. What were her dreams? I'll never know. Anna was never seen again at The Neighborhood Playhouse.

Every minute counted. Martha made sure of that. She was adamant about time. One young man, unavoidably late from Sandy's class, couldn't begin his apology before she hissed at him, "How *dare* you *steal one minute of my life*!"

Martha's always flawless appearance, her demands, admonitions and exhortations, were exhilarating challenges. To please her became my verb. And please her I did. I was a model pupil.

Martha rewarded me with the assignment to choreograph the graduation presentation for our class of 1942. Each year a Broadway theatre was rented, and it was traditional for the school's administrator, Rita Morgenthau, to host a reception afterwards at her Riverside Drive home. I decided to stage nursery rhymes with a sophisticated twist, and directed my actor-classmates to speak while they danced. This reshaped the children's rhymes into wry comment on adult loves, lies, and liaisons.

I hoped my work would please Martha, but after curtain, surrounded by her entourage, she left the theatre without commenting.

Agnes DeMille, who would soon take Broadway into a new era with her choreography for Oklahoma!, came backstage, embraced me, "Saralee this is good choreography, good theatre. You've got it!"

But not a word from Martha.

So I awaited judgement in the excitement of Rita Morgenthau's lavish party.

And Martha swept in, late, formally gowned, ravishing. My gaunt icon in taffeta.

She greeted each person carefully. I waited. At last she stood still. The students pulled back, hushed. Martha looked at me, cocked her head slightly as if she couldn't quite place me. Almost as an afterthought, she spoke my name: "Saralee. You know, for years I've wanted to choreograph those nursery rhymes. Now I don't have to. You've done it. Successfully." I think she smiled. She moved on.

So did I. I abandoned dance in favour of acting. Dance in itself dissatisfied me. But then acting by itself frustrated me. I worked, taught and directed. Martha's single-mindedness was permanently engraved on my memory, and on my work habits. Eventually, through experience and experiment, I was able to meld the two forms, and to create plays with actors dancing and dancers acting, speaking and moving simultaneously. And I found myself reproving latecomers for stealing minutes from my life!

Years later I saw Martha's farewell tour. The leg that had once seemed to brush her ear struggled to rise at all, and then only when she was supported by male dancers. She was her own cadaver, a victim of traumatic and dramatic disappointments, alcohol, face-lifts, and social rounds with wealthy patrons. The simple, powerful movement that had first inspired me was now convoluted and decadent.

I was shaken. Yet I judged her by her own standard. "Movement," she insisted, "never lies."

Pursue Your Verb!

STELLA ADLER WAS TALL, BLOND, AND VERY SERIOUS, leaning forward to have her cigarette lighted. But there was a problem with her hat, a black "chapeau" with a saucy black veil to her chin. It gave her a she-who-must-be-obeyed bearing. She kept trying to push the cigarette through the fragile webbing of the veil, while her producer husband, Harold Clurman, stood by with his gold lighter flaming. Stella cued him with an ever-so-slight nod of her head. Clurman raised the lighter to the cigarette. She huffed and she puffed — to no avail.

Gently, determinedly, Clurman worked Stella's cigarette out of the veil, turned it around so that its now slightly burned cork tip was toward her mouth where it belonged, and reinserted it through the veil.

It had been a wordless scene worthy of Stanislavsky's dictum, *pursue your verb*. She'd pursued her verb to light that cigarette with such purpose that Clurman had no alternative but to give up his role as observer and become involved. She-who-must-be-obeyed had been.

This incidental entr'acte, played out in no more than a minute, burned itself into my memory.

That was 1944. I was an American then. Still Sara Lee *Harris*. I was with another young actor at the Broadway opening of *Harvey*. My boyfriend wanted to be seen during intermission, so quick as a bunny I accompanied him to the lobby. After I got my breath he looked around for producers and directors whose notice he might subtly attract.

The boyfriend nudged me and whispered, "Over there! Stella Adler! Over there!"

I had studied at The Neighborhood Playhouse and knew her name. It was spoken with reverence. Stella Adler was THE authority on the Stanislavsky Method. She'd studied with him in Moscow!

I'd just finished a summer stock stint. It had left me frustrated and irritable after two intensive years at The Neighborhood Playhouse exploring theatre arts — acting, dance, choreography. I'd experienced the driving force of Martha Graham and Louis Horst in movement and composition. I'd been surrounded by ambitious talented colleagues and become aware that there might be a goal for me beyond performing. I'd had that first glimmering hope that I might one day be an authentic theatre artist — a teacher, a director, perhaps a creator.

The summer in stock had been more than jarring; it was shattering. I'd hated the lack of concern among actors and directors in commercial theatre. I wanted to be among creative people; I wanted to learn more. I wanted to study with Stella — forgetting that I'd already had the teacher-of-teachers in Sandy Meisner, who had adroitly adapted the Method techniques learned from Stella. His training had won me a contract with the William Morris Agency and Equity membership by the end of my first year — a coup!

Stella was then teaching a drama workshop at The New School for Social Research. I applied for a scholarship. She granted it. I was eager for Stella's approval. I got it.

No sooner was the workshop underway than the William Morris Agency phoned. Urgent. The USO was casting *You Can't Take It With You* (a Pulitzer Prize winner)! They'd scheduled me for an audition for the role of Essie. I won the part. I was about to be directed by none other than Stella's own brother, the equally remarkable Luther Adler — *if* Stella would release me from the scholarship. She said yes.

I acknowledge the terrible contradiction. I'd run from crass commercial theatre to the cocoon of school. Then, given the chance to enhance my career, I grabbed it and ran back.

I was away from New York for six months and learned to count every one of them. A USO tour of armed forces camps is definitely not glamorous. The wide-eyed aspirant catapulted from the theories of drama school to the actualities of living "theatuh" learns more than how to collect a cheque from the business manager each week: how not to walk on another actor's lines, not to breathe on their laughs, not to upstage or downstage seasoned colleagues (Jack Norworth had the lead in our production: a wry comedian, master of the "throwaway line," and composer of such songs as *Harvest Moon* and *Take Me Out to the Ball Game*), how to fit neatly — and bleakly — into a customary pattern established by an envious histrionic hierarchy. It is every actor's preparation for the big moment — the Broadway Debut.

Stella had a lot to do with mine. She unwittingly arranged it. I phoned her as soon as I came back to New York. She'd been generous in releasing me from my scholarship to do the tour and I wanted to say thank you and perhaps go back to study with her. The day I called she was on her way to rehearsal in "a new and wonderful play, Irwin Shaw's *Sons and Soldiers*." Max Reinhardt was directing and she, Stella Adler, had a "mahvllus" part opposite Gregory Peck and Geraldine Fitzgerald. The simple straightforward teacher I'd known had once again assumed her theatrical persona.

"Dahling, you must come and see me and tell me all about your tour. Just ask the doorman to show you to my dressing room."

The result of my USO tour was a healthy bank account. I was completely unhurried. I didn't hurry uptown but dressed casually in a fresh little Lanz, green and girl-like. I had a delicate lunch at Schrafft's — I could afford it now — and took a double-decker bus up Fifth Avenue to Forty-Seventh Street. It was only my third day back in New York after a half-year absence. It had to be choice.

I knew it might be months or at least weeks before the pressure of rehearsals would start again. I expected to pay the customary calls on agents and producers, audition, read, worry, and live in suspense. I never doubted that it would culminate in a Broadway Debut: although alert observation of languishing unemployed friends should have shaken my unbounded faith.

When I finally sauntered to the stage entrance of the Morosco Theater I was surprised to see a long queue of girls, obviously actresses. They all appeared to be of one mould, tall, seductive, sleek. I walked past the line to the stage door and was stopped by an aggressive young Stage Manager.

"You're not the type, honey," he said.

"I beg your pardon," I meekly answered, "I would like to see Miss —"

"I told you, kid, you're not the type."

Confused and embarrassed, I asked icily, "Why?"

"Why? Cheez!" He turned in disgust from my ponytail and dirndl to answer the telephone.

During his eloquent "yeah, yeahs" and "nah, nahs" I quietly inched up the spiral iron stairs to find Stella.

We greeted each other noisily in the customary theatrical manner. Also in the customary theatrical manner we both talked at once. To keep this going for a quarter of an hour is quite exhausting, and at the end of it we were both willing to observe amenities.

In the first lull I remarked on the Stage Manager's refusal to admit me to Stella's dressing room. Her uncomprehending expression forced me to add, "He had the audacity to say I wasn't the type!"

Stella looked at me long and hard, the way they do in Westerns. Then she broke into perfectly pitched peals of laughter.

"Oh! You're green, dahling! And it's not only your dress! The Stage Manager didn't realize you were looking for me. He thought you were looking for the Girl-in-the-Park role!" Another gale of laughter! "And dahling, you're not the type!"

Stella, the great exponent of Stanislavsky, Stella, the internationally famous teacher of creative acting, was type-casting. *That* struck me as funny!

Now it was my turn to look at her long and hard.

She did a very slow take and then a very fast one.

"OK, dahling, let's see what we can do. Take down your hair. Make like uh, you know ... Mmmm, better. Now lots of lipstick. But that dress. Spring in Salt Lake City. Why don't you buy a sweater? A real red sweater. Hurry."

She shoved some cigarettes, matches, and gum at me as a final suggestion of what the role required, gave me a kiss and pushed me out of her dressing room.

I raced down the stairs, ducked out the alley, headed for a woman's shop, and bought the red sweater. I pulled it on.

Once more I walked to the stage door of *Sons and Soldiers*. I sashayed to the Stage Manager. He seemed perplexed. I smoothed my red sweater. I chewed my gum. With an innocent concentration worthy of Stella Adler I put a cigarette to my mouth and asked him for a light.

He said, "Just a minute, cutie."

I waited.

He came back with two other gentlemen: Max Reinhardt, the Director, and Norman Bel Geddes, the Producer and Scenic Designer. They looked at me carefully.

"Come this way, my dear," Reinhardt said.

Bel Geddes whispered, "She's just the type."

I crossed the mysterious otherworld of backstage. I crossed the threshold of Broadway. Three nights later I made my debut.

It was almost a disaster.

The curtain went up. I was alone, sitting on a park bench. It was night. Three young men sauntered into view and sat on a nearby bench. They did their best to keep their conversation going while I did my best to distract them. The audience enjoyed the by-play, waiting for the real scene to begin. There was an expectant hush in the house. The hush became a gasp as a gigantic shadow slowly descended on the four of us. Norman Bel Geddes' imaginatively designed set was falling inch by inch. My bench faced slightly upstage so I was the first among the actors to see the catastrophe coming. Greg Peck took his cue from the frightened audience. He turned toward me and the descending flats. He walked over to my bench quickly — and much sooner than originally directed. From our two different angles, he standing and I seated, we raised our arms to stop the falling set. Meisner-trained, neither of us missed a beat. We held up Bel Geddes' scenery and brought the house down.

That was my Broadway Debut.

The day that Stella had suggested I buy that red sweater, the day I'd read for Reinhardt and Bel Geddes, the day I was told this small gem of a role was mine, I was bouyant.

Mr. Reinhardt led me toward the footlights to introduce me to the other actors. He didn't have to. Greg came down-stage, leaned over the footlights and said, "I know Sara Lee from The Neighborhood Playhouse. This is great!"

I felt wonderful. He'd been a year ahead of me at The Neighborhood Playhouse. We all knew that he was an up-and-coming star, *assured*, were the rumours, of film and stage contracts. Greg was inscrutable on the subject. He worked extremely hard. We all did, preparing exercises, rehearsing night and day, weekends and holidays. I have an unforgettable image of his strenuous efforts to relax his rigid body, and his speech exercises for resonance. I can still hear his repeated intoning of "honey-money ... honey-money money money ..."

The advanced students performed each Friday for an audience of agents, producers, and directors. We first-year students were encouraged to observe. Greg gave a memorable performance one week.

He went all out to apply THE METHOD. In his scene he was to arrive onstage out of breath, so he raced down two flights of stairs and right back up again, arriving just in time to make his entrance, look at his fellow actors, and collapse.

Greg was always the gentleman, kind, rather distant, pleasantly friendly to me. When I'd returned from my USO European jaunt, the William Morris Agency sent me to the coast for a screen test with Warner Brothers. I took courage in hand and phoned Greg — courage because Greg by now was big-time. But we had studied together, we had held up Bel Geddes' set together, and New York friends encouraged me to contact him — in fact had given me his home phone number. (They wanted a full report on his doings as a star.)

He was surprised when I reached him, warm, glad to hear from a Playhouse friend and Broadway colleague. He invited me to visit, meet his wife, and have dinner. The next day he called back, tripping over platitudes: " … forgotten a previous commitment … I'll be in touch." He never was.

I wasn't hurt but my ego was slightly crushed. I thought, maybe his wife (the first one) just doesn't want to entertain an uninfluential aspiring actress; perhaps someone had informed someone that Sara Lee Harris had known Isa and other Russians, that she had studied with Stella who had studied with Stanislavsky — another Russian. The witch hunt was just beginning but was already the biggest game in town.

I did not get to work with Stella Adler again. But my Broadway Debut has a special place in my heart for one particular reason: in the imposing Cast of Characters that publishers print before the text, my name is not listed for any of the productions in which I performed on Broadway or on tour, with the single exception of *Sons and Soldiers*. In *The Skin of Our Teeth*, *Snafu*, *Boy Meets Girl*, etcetera, I was always the replacement, the bridesmaid the directors reassured me was more beautiful than the bride! But in Irwin Shaw's play, published by Random House, you will see "Marie (the Girl in the Park): . . . . Sara Lee Harris."

Walk-Ons and Bit-Parts

THE STAGE WAS PARTIALLY LIGHTED, just bright enough for me to audition for the role of Gladys in Thornton Wilder's Pulitzer Prize winner, *The Skin of Our Teeth*. I was welcomed by the once-celebrated director, Mr. Arthur Hopkins, pinch-hitting for the play's actual but absent director, Elia Kazan. Before giving me the script, Mr. Hopkins suggested I might like to meet Mr. Wilder's sister.

The dark split. Isabel popped up. A perky hat capped her small figure and with a bright smile she grasped my hand. "We want this to be good for Thornton," she said. Her little lisp and friendly puckered mouth under the perky hat bespoke Bugs Bunny.

I read two scenes and got the contract to play Gladys, the innocent, fact-devouring daughter, and to understudy the role of the sexy, man-devouring Sabina. Isabel was charmed by me and I was charmed by her. And excited. I played Gladys for two weeks on Broadway and packed my trunk for Boston. It was our first — and last — opening of the coast-to-coast grand tour!

The star who took over Tallulah Bankhead's role was a terrific actor and a terrific alcoholic, so far gone by opening night that a replacement had to be rushed from New York. There'd been no chance for me to have a run-through in the role as the official understudy. I was out of a play but not out of contact with Isabel.

In Boston she treated me to the traditional Swanboat Ride to prepare me for the play's closing. In New Haven she took me to lunch at the Yale Faculty Club and expressed her contempt for Ross Lockeridge's *Raintree County* — which Thornton shared of course — and she added that she and T. were elated that Ernest Hemingway had received the Nobel Prize: "Thornton thinks it's long overdue." She quoted her brother generously. She became my friend.

"We want this to be good for Thornton." That was Isabel Wilder's life. Thornton's successes were hers; his friends were hers — Gertrude Stein and Alice B., Tallulah Bankhead and

Ruth G. (for Gordon). Her life was a window pane through which on clear days she looked out on a world celebrating him. On foggy days her hand rubbed quiet circles across the glass so that Thornton could see a single leaf.

He must not see the fog when lunch was ready. She cooked quietly from recipes created by the far-off Toklas in Paris. (And later, much later, made me a Christmas present of Alice B. Toklas' recipe book, inscribed of course). She polished silently so that no sound would interrupt his work. Thornton had his food alone on a tray in his study. Isabel had hers alone in the bright kitchen where she hung paper towels to dry. There would be no waste; a special drawer was set aside for string. The Wilders could have afforded a cook, a laundress, a cleaning woman, but Thornton went to pieces if anyone other than his sister made the tiniest noise. In short, those painful discs in Thornton's spine gave his sister Isabel a never-ending backache.

To and fro to Europe she must go, arranging, packing, emptying closets and chiffoniers for whatever trustworthies would rent "the-house-*The-Bridge*-built" (it was built on Deepwood Drive, New Haven, Connecticut, to celebrate the success of Thornton's novel, *The Bridge of San Luis Rey*), so often temporarily vacant. There was England, of course, and Paris. And Germany, once the war was over and so many royalties awaited.

I don't know if Thornton ever knew James Joyce but he certainly took Joyce's prescription for writers to heart: demand "silence, exile, and cunning." He got all three through his sister.

Isabel may have published one or two forgettable novels, but the one that was to have been THE book — the book she'd been writing and writing — was lost in the silence she could never win, in the exile that kept her busily tracking their social and business obligations, and in the economic cunning she could muster only for her brother.

Her own book, THE book, was scattered. Parts of it were left in London and "dear friend Max Beerbohm must help retrieve it." It was never found. Later, much later, years later, all her cards, notes, and letters spoke of trying to piece it together. I still don't have the faintest idea what it was about.

In all this turbulence she found time for correspondence. Her handwriting is hurried, often almost illegible. It demands re-reading — several times! Whole words are left unfinished, stretched out like laundry lines. They were always of Thornton: "*T. has just finished correcting the galley of his book which will be out in Oct. The work was very hard on his one useable eye. We can't wait to get back home ... he's so unwell ...*"; another: "*T. has been very ill ... a change is ordered. We sail today for Europe. I'll write as soon as I can.*"

She found the strength to be considerate of friends. There was an invitation to view the French film, *La Ronde*. I was impressed with its movement from naturalism to abstraction, its breaking from the customary camera form. Isabel remarked bitterly, "Thornton introduced this style. It was Thornton, but they don't give him any credit for this." Wistfully, sadly, she repeated it.

One afternoon she invited me to see Gide's *The Immoralist* with the up-and-coming James Dean. During intermission I audibly expressed my enthusiasm for the play's bold handling of homosexuality. In 1954! Isabel shushed me, giggling nervously, and murmured a warning to behave.

Her unvarying politeness, like her unobtrusive but feminine suits and ensembled hats, covered a multitude of excuses for Thornton and his friends. Always her high-pitched, quivering voice nervously excused, explained, commented, inquired. Like her handwriting, her talk was rushed and incomplete.

Once Isabel asked me if she should marry a French Professor — or a prof. who was French. She knelt on the floor, having placed me on an antique needlepoint stool to measure my hemline. All her Deepwood Drive neighbours, tree-ensconced, had been asked, too. I was impressed more by her expert seamstress' skills than by her marriage proposal. She smiled wryly through a mouthful of pins and viewed her handiwork. Middle-aged spinster nervously stammering admiration for my petite "figure." ("Body" a word reserved for physicians, was not used in needlepointed parlours — like "homosexual.")

"Sure, Isabel," I said to myself, "marry the man. Everyone is urging you to take the bull [to myself I think, *any* bull] by the horns." At the same time I'm thinking: Balls!

Isabel giggled, pulled the pins out of her mouth, and ran to answer the phone. She hurried back radiant with joy. "Sara Lee," she cried, "Thornton's brother — our brother—Amos has been appointed to Harvard's Theology Department!" Before I could complete my congratulations she was back at my hemline.

I went back to the subject: "Well, will you marry him?"

She tilted her head, squinted her blue eyes, gauged my skirt length, leaned backwards looking up at me like a nun looking at Michelangelo's David, and sputtered, "No."

Sometimes when she was telling me about her pivotal role in the family, and especially in Thornton's life, her resentment twanged like a tuning fork long after our conversation ended.

"Somebody has to pay for another's success." I distinctly remember her saying that. "There's always somebody!" It was clear that Isabel "thought" about independence, but by the time I knew her she had assumed an almost joyous martyrdom as secretary, emissary, nurse, and even, I hazard, unwanted companion to Thornton, rolling under the boulder of responsibilities like a reverse Sysiphus, allowing herself to be crushed only with the finality of Thornton's death.

When I played Gladys in *The Skin of Our Teeth* on Broadway Isabel came backstage, hugged me and said, "At last Gladys is being performed the way my brother envisioned her. It's that third act when Gladys becomes a mother that brings her character to full life. I believed that you were actually handling a *real* baby." She was ecstatic. "That was Thornton's intention, Sara Lee, to emphasize the family as the ongoing nucleus of civilization."

She hinted more than once that "family" and "survival" were themes rooted in the Wilders' experience; a tyrannical authoritarian father, a determined self-sacrificing mother, and five independent-minded children created centripetal and centrifugal forces of loyalty and rebellion. Over this whirlpool of passion, imagination, and ambition hovered a troubling threat.

One rainy weekend when Thornton was away I was invited to visit. Isabel was thoughtfully, quite silently preparing some complicated confection. I looked on in envious admiration. She turned to me, her voice low. "My sister Charlotte," she barely whispered, "the most brilliant of us all, a genius, a fantastic genius ... she went to pieces ... mad ... she's away ... put away."

Isabel decided that I was trustworthy, and so for nine months in 1955-56 I rented their home on Deepwood Drive in New Haven, Connecticut. The room where Thornton worked — one might loosely label it the library — is still vivid in memory. That workroom became my familiar: the old large desk, threadbare carpet and furniture, the lumpy couch Thornton rested on between bouts of writing in longhand while standing at his lectern. It became my workroom for my studies at Yale. I loved the huge dictionary mounted on that lectern, and discovered in its leaves innumerable slips of paper with Thornton's notes on them. Why did I resist the temptation to pocket them?

Deepwood Drive was a comfortable cottage-like rambling place, deep in the wood, overlooking a ravine, lovely in the autumn when the leaves were falling, constructed on many levels in the days before "split-level," built in relation to the terrain, painted a dark rich brown, melding into the forest around it.

Isabel enjoyed telling me stories about that house. Another room remains in my memory, a tiny one that Isabel favoured. It had an extremely hard, extremely narrow bed. Isabel slept there when her back was bothering her. It seems Laurence Olivier and Vivien Leigh also preferred that bed. They'd visited Thornton in preparation for their London run of *The Skin of Our Teeth*. "They insisted!" Isabel giggled, "on sleeping in that narrow thing instead of using our twin-bedded guest room! I warned them that there'd be no room to turn over! But they insisted!"

There were stories of Thornton and Tallulah Bankhead enjoying late, exhausting nights after curtain in New Haven, exchanging barbed anecdotes and polishing off a bottle of bourbon — " A whole bottle, Sara Lee!" Then Sabina would lunge down those steep wooden stairs to a waiting taxi, brandishing the empty bourbon bottle, refusing her escort's help, declaiming unprintable exit lines. At three-thirty in the morning the taxi driver was impatient. Isabel gave him Tallulah's address, Thornton waved hilarious farewell and went to bed. Isabel cleaned up.

* * * * *

It is through Isabel's telescope that I view Thornton. I see him distant but clear in the lens she kept so meticulously polished. I never met Thornton on Broadway, nor had the commercial relationship with him that other actors had: Ruth Gordon, his Dolly in *The Matchmaker*, or Tallulah Bankhead, who was his definitive Sabina in *Skin*. My first meeting with him was in Caserta, Italy, during W.W.II — without Isabel present.

Hundreds of us were stationed in the monstrous summer palace of Italy's last king—liaison officers, journalists, entertainers, passing politicians, and us. Four women. Actors. Not just entertainers! The very first troupe (we were the USO's guinea pigs) to perform full-length American plays at the front lines. I was considered a fairly good theatre property, having been noticed in several Broadway productions. A sergeant temporarily in charge of our Fifth Army unit had heard that I'd already been featured in *Skin*. He was busting to direct another of Wilder's works, *Our Town*, with me as Emily, and suggested I meet with Thornton.

"Maybe we can get his permission to stage it as part of our tour."

"Meet Thornton Wilder? We're in a war zone!"

Well, so was Thornton. That was a surprise! Intelligence units were stationed in the recesses of the king's palace, all unknown to us actresses. Thornton Wilder was part of one of them.

The sergeant led me through a labyrinth of corridors, up and down swirling stairways, past questioning guards, and into the belly of this whale of a building.

Thornton expected us. His door opened as freely as his smile. "O! How right you are for Emily!" He greeted me and invited me to chat. Isabel had written him glowingly of my Gladys. He promised to do everything possible to get *Our Town* released, but warned that his agents might be reluctant for the USO to have it before it premiered commercially. He rose as I was leaving, clasped my hand impulsively, and, referring to the drug store scene in *Our Town*, said, "When you get back home, Emily, have a strawberry phosphate for me!"

In my memory, Thornton is effervescent, bubbling with life. His intense *joie de vivre* and rapidity of speech made his words ping.

My next meeting with him was even more memorable. It happened long after the war, during my tenancy at Deepwood Drive. His latest play, *The Alcestiad*, or *A Life in the Sun*, had just been produced at the Edinburgh Festival. On the ship coming back to New York, Thornton had been altering it, working out his dissatisfactions. From shipboard he'd wired his neighbours to gather for a reading with criticism, and asked them particularly to include me. We met at the home of

William Sloane Coffin's mother (the same William S.C. later involved in the infamous Dan Berrigan-Vietnam episode).

I was so excited about the entire event that I don't recall what was said about the play itself! I felt insecure, too. I'd read an English translation of the original Greek work to prepare for the evening. But as I listened to Thornton's version, I thought it dry, academic, not "actable." I also felt myself to be intellectually inferior and that any contribution I might make would be, if not ridiculed—these people were too polite for rudeness—ridiculous. Yet Thornton asked for and listened to my comments with genuine appreciation. The good teacher.

What most impressed me was Thornton's delight with the occasion. He loved to act and he read aloud most, if not all, the parts.

After the reading he apologized for not having come to call for me. I hadn't expected him to. He'd rushed straight from the ship to New Haven for this first reading of his new play in the States and was hurtling back to New York that night. Still, he earnestly apologized for not having brought me to the affair personally! He asked if he might make up for his oversight by escorting me home.

So we walked to Deepwood Drive together. It was a beautiful night. He intertwined my arm with his, became Mr. Antrobus to my Gladys. Perfect father-daughter. He looked up to the sky, squeezed my hand, and started,

Star light star bright ...

and we skipped together, actually skipped along as we finished,

... we wish we may,
we wish we might,
have the wish
we wish tonight.

After the war, while I was taking courses at Yale, I was asked to play Arkadina in Chekhov's *The Seagull*. As a result of that, Dean Canfield, the new Drama Department Chair, wired Thornton in Europe to ask if *The Matchmaker* would be available. He wanted to cast me as Dolly. Thornton made the effort, but his agents, Brandt & Brandt, argued that, while I was Actors' Equity, the Yale students who would play with me were not and therefore — at that time — not "pro." The play wasn't available for amateur rights.

Thornton believed himself sensitive and open to all the arts. Yet some years after I'd moved on and was receiving some acclaim for my synthesis of acting and dance, I wrote and asked him for permission to adapt his novel, *The Bridge of San Luis Rey*, for this theatre form I was developing. In that gentle way he had, he curiously revealed that he was a purist about dance:

May 10, 1960

Dear Sara Lee,

Please don't be disappointed — and please don't get mad.

I've vetoed all dramatization of Bridge and all working on it as an opera (tho' one got by me in Germany during the war and is being staged there) because simultaneous stories simply don't work on the stage. (I don't care what they do to it in the movies and TV, but I've noticed it doesn't work there either.) [According to Isabel he was horrified and humiliated by the cinema version of *Our Town*.] ... *I've had to refuse to other choreographers and shall probably have to refuse it again.*

Besides, — tho' it has nothing to do with the above "meanness" — I love dancing when it has the least story to tell and when its least mixed up in other forms. I love it when Balanchine sets them to sheer patterns and I hate it when he asks us to follow The Prodigal Son and The Seven Deadly Sins with Lotta Lenya singing while I'm trying to look. And we were the other afternoon at Martha Graham:

wonderful when angels were playing endless games, and oh so hard-to-follow when Martha was writhing about as one or the other of the tortured Greek heroines — Jocasta or Clytemnestra.

Isabel benefited from her trip south and is pretty well. She will be writing to you, too, and — I hope — asking you to forgive me.

A world of regards.
Ever,
Thornton.

I asked Thornton's advice about a short story that a major literary agent had rejected because, while he thought it was good, it was not "mainstream." Thornton was sincerely concerned:

June 10, 1960

Dear Sara Lee,

The letter from the agent is well expressed. It lacks one thing. If he thinks so highly of the story he could have recommended the names of several reviews that might consider it favourably. He could have gone one step further and said: "We're only in the large-circulation business. We only handle stories that can get from $500 to $2,000 dollars, from which we get our 15%.... "

He was concerned enough to include a list of "small" reviews that paid thirty to fifty dollars, and went on to say what he felt an honest agent would have told me:

" ... we haven't time to mention them, and it would make us uncomfortable to read them...."

If you write that kind of story I don't think it worth your while to take his advice and slant your work toward the BIG MARKET. You'd only harm yourself and probably wouldn't be able to make it even if you tried. Banal stories are written by banal minds, and readers can "smell" it when a superior writer tries to stoop to please them.

devotedly ever,
Thornton.

* * * * *

I was a walk-on in Thornton and Isabel Wilder's lives. At the time, their natural kindness made it seem a featured role.

They were to me like advancing and receding waves leaving foam and tangled seaweed on the shores of my life yet never obliterating my aimless footprints. Their life was rational because their needs were rational, long-term; mine were chaotic, capricious.

Intermission with Five Minutes to Spare

1943:
There was a war going on. Many of my friends and family were already in it and I worried about them, but for me the promise of a thrilling stage career overshadowed everything.

I gaily bounced from one ingenue role to another, usually as a featured replacement. I kept hoping for a bigger something, not quite certain of the something I wanted. I did know that the naive charm I exuded onstage was belied by the restlessness I felt offstage.

In those days the market was flooded with aspiring young actresses, yet I was never without work longer than two or three weeks. A singular situation. How was it, then, that I grabbed an offer to join the USO's new overseas unit in the North African-European theatre?

Theatre is for adventurers. I wanted the chance to travel beyond the borders of the United States and this was a winner. I was fearful of moving into combat zones, but the United States Service Organization assured me that I would be well out of danger in North Africa. Italy was not on the entertainment agenda while our forces were still fighting for a foothold there.

Our unit of four women was to pioneer the first legitimate full-length plays for the American troops. We would be joined by soldiers from the rest areas who had previously been professional actors.

I would open our tour in *Boy Meets Girl*, playing the title role I'd recently revived on Broadway. My life became a series of exclamation points — adventure! travel! career!

* * * * *

Port of Embarkation Quantico, Virginia:
I'm lying shivering on a damnably hard cot in a very cold barracks, a huge hollow barn-like affair. My three colleagues and I, faint from an inoculation administered by barely trained GI medics, have our cots lined up side by side trying

to recover while nurses and vaudeville entertainers are establishing their priorities.

The nurses are all business, efficiently sorting and packing their duffel bags. The entertainers are tuning instruments and trading cigarettes; one of them plays an accordion, accompanying a tap dancer. Ginny, Siddy, Brooke, and I make it clear we are annoyed. Definitely no part of their entourage. We turn our backs. I pull the blanket over my head willing to suffer its coarse discomfort as a signal for them to cease and desist. To no avail. The steel staccato tapping continues on the bare wood floor. O my head! The whine of the accordion alternates between gasping and wheezing. Our determined entertainers won't give up. If "Tea for Two" won't do it, how about "Roll Out the Barrel"? "Yeah," somebody belts, "let's have a barrel of fun!" "Yeah, the boys loved that in Arkansas!" Now the nurses are giving their whole-hearted attention to singing what the boys loved in Arkansas—and Missouri, Texas, New Jersey and points east!

I get up. OK, I'll contribute to the war effort. Staggering toward the leader of the band, I say, I'll do a striptease if you know "Shimmy Like My Sister Kate," positive they are as ignorant of that old burlesque-house chestnut as I am of the mechanics of a striptease. But without dropping a beat they swing into it. I have to accept the challenge. I kick off my shoes, throw my newly-acquired uniform jacket in the air, wiggle my hips, bump and grind to whistles and catcalls from the nurses. They shout and clap, "Take it off, take it off!" My so-sedate colleagues are doubled over laughing, shrieking taunts: "Stanislavsky never taught you that!" "Is that the Martha Graham bump and grind?" I lift my skirt with ostentatious shyness, undo a purloined silk stocking from my garter belt. "Ooooo, where did *you* get a *silk* stocking my-o-my-o-my!" The place is jumping. I have retrieved the honour of our unit. They are proud of me. I am proud of me, and frankly, to my surprise, I am proud to be one of these gutsy women. Going,

going, and almost gone, I collapse on my cot. No sheets, just a mattress-cover, and a pillowcase, but what the hell! The Bridal Suite at the Waldorf-Astoria could never feel this good.

We simmer down. Siddy, our competent one, tells us authoritatively to sew on our USO insignia. At that moment Star Tap Dancer runs interference: "Be sure to sew the insignia on with double thread, tight, good, because I've been told our insignia is a BADGE OF PROTECTION IN CASE WE'RE CAPTURED WE WON'T BE TORTURED! See? We rate like captains. The League of Nations says so!" Big joke! (But she's serious and the first seeds of fear are planted.)

We become active, cooperating to keep morale high. We sing "We're In the Army Now," slicing through the winter wind to the outdoor latrine. We teach each other: I give barre exercises, the nurses demonstrate First Aid, the entertainers play hit songs and challenge us to supply the lyrics — "Don't Get Around Much Anymore"; "Sentimental Journey" — fluent linguist Ginny doggedly tries us with French. We hit the sack singing, "Over there, over there ... The Yanks are coming." Aren't we, girls?

Our orders come. We are to sail on the *S.S. Anderson.*

It is dark, late, cold. We get on board, are assigned bunk beds row upon row in close quarters barely divided by narrow aisles. I, being the smallest of our unit, am persuaded to take the top tier. I don't like it. I'm too near the ceiling, find it hard to breathe, don't dare be a poor sport, don't dare complain, close my eyes to the bright lights, which do not remind me of Broadway. Tomorrow is lifeboat drill. Remember, Sara Lee, you're a damn good swimmer.

I wish the entertainers would shut up, dry up, or whatever one does on the high seas. They're drowning us in a loud duet of "Tuxedo Junction": "Feelin' low, rockin' slow, want to go right back where I belong ... " The contralto says, "You know girls, we could be torpedoed. But not to worry. The boys told me we've got enough ammunition to protect us."

That word again.

I land in the sick bay crippled with muscle spasms. I'm in uniform. The bland, quiet doctor asks me to take it off, but this isn't a striptease. I explain the spasms are in my chest, I can't breathe. He says he needs to do a thorough check-up before prescribing medication, gently touches my stomach, runs his hands over my legs. Then he invites his young assistant to observe while I lie supine, says I need an injection to completely relax, shows the assistant the procedure for "this type of case." They eye each other unblinkingly. The doctor doesn't jab the needle into my hip, but inserts it, murmurs, "Takes experience."

I say I'm cold, doctor chuckles, so does his assistant. Why are they smirking, or do I only imagine the youngster, almost a kid, salivating? I am sleepy, very, can't keep my eyes open, try to force my lids open, try to sit up but am helpless. I hear myself slurring no, no, stop please. My head keeps dropping back on the table, I can only watch, see vaguely as the two men sway over me in slow motion. Against my will they enter me, penetrate me without a sound, except for my incoherent mumbling that dies, dies away. I feel nothing. I'm out.

No one near me when I wake up. Light is coming through the porthole. It's morning. I take the blanket off, slowly dress, walk past a man I've never seen before. He has a medical insignia on his arm, stripes on his epaulet. He says good morning but I don't answer, keep walking, find my way back to our cabin.

Ginny, Siddy, and Brooke don't believe my whispered story. Rape in the sick bay? They pat my shaking shoulders, give me a hug or two, exchange knowing smiles, chalk up my overnight stay to hysteria and that alarming "Tuxedo Junction" the USO vaudevillian sings incessantly.

Stay with me, I'll unchain the door: I have the childhood key, we can't play games any longer, no more peek-a-boo. I see me. If they didn't believe me it couldn't be true, could it?

Never happened, isn't real. The quiet insistent/persistent rape on the troopship.

A year later I receive a relative home on leave from the Navy. Into my tiny one-room apartment I unfold a cot that will only fit next to my own narrow bed that I proudly offer him. We enjoy swapping stories, he from his bloody Guadalcanal stint, I from my raucous adventures in North Africa and Italy. Soon we tire, lights out, but by Christ! he keeps murmuring. Now it's about Egypt. What is my opinion of their ancient — or is it current — custom of sex within the family? Incest was very much *in* in those days. I'm weary but something tells me to listen, be alert. He turns toward my nearby cot, hand outstretched, fingers reaching. I smother my terror and slither under my cot and spend the night on the floor in rigid silence. Neither next morning nor in later years did either of us allude to his overture or to my disappearance and houdini-like reappearance from under that cot.

After all, my mother was mistress of the mask and I can take on her persona in the wink of an eye.

So now ...

Algeria:
We disembark at Oran. Solid earth under my feet. I stamp, jump, make sure it's real. We're here. "The woild's my erster!" I shout in my broadest Brooklynese, add, "And we're duh poils!" I race Ginny and Brooke to the waiting open truck. Siddy's usual smiling self sidles up to the GI chauffeur, makes sure our luggage is stowed properly.

We drive, we careen, we bump through Gauguin landscape, purple and orange hills, winding patched roads, stretching sea on the left, and on the right hut-shaped houses white among dazzling greenery and the pungent smell of roadside flowers. It's spring! God's so much in his heaven that I can't take my eyes off the sky, excitedly point to it, mistake the pale disc of sun for the moon to roars of laughter from my joshing companions.

At Base Camp we're billeted in tents for the first time and introduced to a bewildering group of eager officers in the Mess. They vie for places next to each of us. Their battle plan is to take turns, change place with every course. Musical Chairs gone berserk! Four prizes in question but none to be retrieved. We four are saving the big bang for the big time to come.

We move from Oran to cosmopolitan Algiers. Ginny and I decide to souk-hunt. We come face to face with two scurrying women in *jihab*, entirely veiled except for their eyes. They giggle, point at us, their eyes mischievously commenting, these foreign women who bare their legs! We point at them, too, in fun, and all four of us laugh. It's friendly and female.

We're in a jeep driven by a native. We go around Algiers in circles. There's Ginny, the European-educated natural blonde of the violet eyes, Eleanor, called Siddy for reasons unknown to me (she's our USO group leader, the "mature one," has a few strands of silvered hair), and Brooke of the spectacular legs.

I can't wait to rehearse *Boy Meets Girl*, in which I play Girl, of course. But now we can't get started. Brooke has become deathly ill. There is considerable turmoil. Siddy is concerned, Ginny is thoughtful, I'm puzzled. I'm also frightened. Is it contagious? I just want to get on with rehearsals, get on stage and do the job I came to do. I want my applause. I make an obligatory call on Brooke in the room she shares with Siddy. It is dark. I stand at the foot of the bed much more irritated than sympathetic. The opening of *Boy Meets Girl* has been delayed! I don't know what to say. I flee.

* * * * *

Whirlwinds are different from siroccos, I learned. The tour had caught me up in a maddening series of clip-shots: barracks, tents, strangers, friends, pain and shocks. I'd been buffeted on my own little axis, but now North Africa's dry wind blew away interferences, swept me up in the adventurous life I understood.

Rehearsals were intense when they finally got underway. Opening night of *Boy Meets Girl* was a smash hit. Here once again audiences responded to me. I might not have been able to find words to speak to Brooke when she lay suffering, but I was always able to light a stage with words written for me.

Applause every night at the packed Opera House in Algiers was crowned with shouts for "Susie, Susie," my role. Walking soldiers and wounded soldiers came to the footlights. "We've never seen round actors before." The more sophisticated sent so many bouquets to our hotel rooms that they overflowed into our bathtubs and bidets. Home was never like this! I was a star in my own firmament, learning to shine as my own sweet self again, even increasing my vocabulary with foreign words: sirocco, bidet. This is the life!

But there were shadows, damn it. We had to visit field hospitals filled with casualties from the Italian Front, look at broken bodies and smell the overwhelming stench of blood. It was easier to pay tribute to the men when I was hidden behind stage makeup or being entertained evenings after the play by American and French officers. The officers made us their pets, intrigued me especially with their big names, celebrities in those days — Douglas Fairbanks Jr., Jean Gabin, the European megastar, John Garfield (that era's Hollywood Lover) and the fascinating Comte De Guise, whose name rang bells from Charlemagne to Charles de Gaulle. (In fluent French, Ginny and the Count arranged for themselves a secret visit to André Gide. I'd have liked to have been included, having been taken by Isabel Wilder to see the then unknown James Dean in Gide's *The Immoralist*, but I discovered their plan too late.)

The daytime inevitably followed: I saw more wounded, more pain, heard more wretched moaning. My sleep was troubled but the curtain could be drawn, to rise again on my comedic *tour de force*.

Then I learned that we were going to where the wounded had come from. Memory humiliates me.

The Special Services Officer gives us the scoop: our unit's been posted — post-haste — to the Italian Front. Finally my discomfort can't be avoided. I am afraid to be wounded. I do not want to be killed. I want out. I argue. I'm chicken. I cannot bear discordant sounds. Anything from the scrape of metal to the slamming of a door makes me frantic, makes me scream, pound on walls, shout obscenities. How will I survive the screech of a dive bomber, crackling ack-ack? I'll break down in front of everybody if there's a bombardment!

Captain Brown cajoles, wheedles, threatens: Do you want to be sent home in disgrace? A coward? OK. I am a coward. I'm also afraid that people will find out, my Marine brother in the Pacific, my paratrooper husband. Chin in, shoulders straight, I suck my gut in and go.

* * * * *

How does one resume a love affair that has been disrupted so many times, had so many ups and downs?

Was it a he? Many. Should they be described for identification? Impossible. Different, identical, similar uniforms, they were in and out so fast I hardly had a chance to see. I wrote my mother, "Oh flying is such fun! I just want to sing and whistle. I hope to fly home!!!"

My sexy, traumatic affair with airplanes lasted over fifty years. It began with my first flight, a World War II bomber going from Algeria to Italy with just our unit of four actresses and a gorgeous South African pilot. Gorgeous and hostile. He was blond, white, did not like being involved in this war. A democratic win was, for him, a threat to his white supremacy.

My interest wasn't political. I was thrilled to be up in the air, walking all over God's heaven. I couldn't sit still, had no intention of remaining in a bucket seat. I managed to get close enough to Gorgeous George to see through the glass bubble of the turret. I felt like an angel soaring over the fabled blue-green Mediterranean. Flying never became routine; it was always exciting.

When our unit was transferred, we were given a free weekend. I spent mine with Bill, my English Major.

Rome:
It's good to get into a real bed, single though it may be, having slept on nothing but canvas cots since coming to Italy. I'm tired. We gave a fast-paced performance of a stupid comedy, *Out of the Frying Pan*, for a much-too-appreciative audience evenly divided between GIs and officers — the officers hogging the front rows.

I snuggle between clean sheets, am falling asleep. A crazy tune keeps whistling through my head: "Who's that knocking at my door, who's that knocking at my door? ... Barnacle Bill, the sailor!" I lie on my back, stretching, smiling ... That ain't no Barnacle Bill, that's Major Bill, my English officer. My Bill. Tall, crinkly blue eyes, broad straight mouth over surprisingly good teeth for an Englishman. Haven't seen him for an entire day. "Don't miss me too much, Honey." (He adores parroting that Americanism learned from me when we first made love.)

"I have to stay close to the Big Brass tonight," he says, "waiting to hear the gen." (I like his Britishism for the American scuttlebutt.) "There may be promotions." My Major Bill has served four years in the "bloody war." He wants a change, any kind of change, higher rank, more pips.

Poor Barnacle, I think. No, Bill. I drift off to sleep. Almost. Wish Bill were here but he's at a party for the upper echelon. Hmmn, yawn, sleep. My room faces the square, the notorious *Quattro Fontani*, where the Nazis had viciously pulled men, women, and children from their beds a few months ago. Shot them in retaliation for sabotage by the Resistance. My bedroom is two stories above the fountains.

It's late, very late, all is silent when scratch, scratch, scratch. I sit bolt upright. O God, not mice, or worse, rats! Plop, plop, then again scratch. This time I hear a faint beating against the drainpipe outside my window. And there's the sweetest humming, a few sounds like — singing? A giggle. A whoops! And scratch, and thump, and plop; "There'll be bluebirds over the white cliffs of —" hiccup. "Sara, Sara," soft but clear now. "Sara!" Bill's mellifluous voice. "Sara," fierce whisper, lots of giggling, scraping on the drainpipe, then those questing blue eyes directly above my window sill. I stealthily open the window. Bill's chin is over the ledge but he's too many sheets to the wind. "Let me in, Sara," he stage-whispers. I grab his hands and together we reach, pull, and pull again, boisterous as we land him, all six feet of him, cap rakishly askew. "Salute me," he says; "I'm now Lieutenant Colonel William H. Hughes, I want you to be the first to know!" We roll on the floor gasping, joyously clasped together.

Rome is my fairyland. We spend many hours of Bill's free time walking, I ogling what's already familiar to him, an Oxford scholar: a panorama of arches, bridges, monuments, winding streets that now shelter hidden shops, whose black market silks, laces, scarves I covet, alluring "civvies" to relieve the regulation blue uniformed days and costumed nights. We buy surreptitiously to take back home when my tour is over. There's a filmy peach nightgown wrung from a sultry salesgirl who yields it resentfully to my British colonel at a price too low to be haggled, a bookstore's enchanting window where Bill loses no time buying me a tiny edition of Dante's *Vita Nuova*, I who only know the name Dante as an awe-inspiring poet to be read at some future date when there might be time.

There is the Hotel Excelsior on the Via Veneto where we, the privileged, eat Spam disguised with exquisite epicurean ingenuity by hungry, creative Italian chefs on whom Allied officers shower favours, bribe or intimidate.

And there's the Vatican, St. Peter's which bores me with overstuffed pomposity, the place where Bill and I have our one and only furious fight. He wants to linger over tombs shrouded in histories of which I am ignorant.

"Do you *mind*," he snaps, "if I look at King Charles? He was an Englishman!"

I detest the dead, need the excitement of the swirling city, living people.

"Who gives a damn about King Charles!"

I turn on my neat little heels, ashamed of my ignorance, flee outside quite lost in the mighty colonnaded rotunda. Bill doesn't follow. Suddenly I spy an old friend, *Herald-Tribune* journalist Russell Hill.

"Russ," I grin, "can I thumb a ride back to the Excelsior?"

"Oh s-sure Sara Lee, but first I h-have to c-cover the P-pope's press conference. In the S-S-Sistine Chapel. You want t-to come with m-m-me?"

My heart is touched by Russ' handsome face and stuttering speech. So I go. We have to rush, Russ is running late, but gentleman that he always is, he never lets go of my hand. He flashes his press pass and brooks no questions about my lack of credentials. We take wrong turnings, get lost in long slippery corridors. Out of breath we finally find an enormous set of doors barred by two Swiss guards, their sharp axe-bladed halberds crossed in an X. We slide to a stop. We stare at them, still holding hands, breathing hard. They stare straight ahead. Russ flashes his ID. They uncross their halberds, the doors open inward.

We gasp, stand motionless. The Sistine Chapel is filled with startled guests. Every head turns to look at us. Enthroned in unearthly white at the top of the aisle sits Pope Pius XII, Giacometti-thin, so weightless it seems he might levitate. He is breathtaking! The entire assemblage, black- and scarlet-robed prelates, press corps, diplomats, is hushed in anticipation of whatever it is they think we are going to do next. Russ' hand squeezes mine. He sputters, "J-J-esus Christ S-sara Lee, Th-Th-They're g-going to m-m-m-marry us!"

* * * * *

I had to catch up with my unit for rehearsal Monday morning. Bill, in command of area transportation, got me on a flight. His batman chauffeured me to the airfield, where an American officer countermanded my reservation, said I could not defy regulations. This flight was strictly VIP. I'd have to hitch another. But there wasn't another. This one was my last chance. The loyal batman phoned Bill, told him I looked "upset." British understatement. I was in a panic. Bill dropped everything, rushed to the airfield and diplomatically pulled rank.

I flew off with the well-heeled and peripatetic Archbishop Spellman of New York, Chief Chaplain of the United States Forces. We were both in the same business: his job was to bless the boys, cheer them on to murder and maim God's enemies, mine was to entertain them while they did it.

He made room for me in his entourage. You might say I joined a religious community in Italy's rarified atmosphere. The Archbishop and his crusaders busied themselves with their prayer books, rapidly turning pages marked with gaily coloured satin ribbons. I didn't interrupt their celestial progress, but kept my eyes riveted on my poor offering, Stanislavsky's *An Actor Prepares*.

Spellman graciously gave me one of the two upholstered seats, while his pissed-off secretary joined the other bucket-seated priests. Darn it! They were so good-looking! No question about it, the sky was the limit.

Somewhere between Rome and Bologna, the Archbishop's fatherly hand, very white and unused but for a jewelled signet ring, pointed to the gutted green landscape below. What did he want me to see — the corruption of God's creation or the achievement of our Allied Forces? He never said.

There was a stirring as we descended. Smooth as cream the plane landed. The Archbishop and his bevy of boys stood, gathered their attaché cases and moved toward the door. But not before I'd managed to insert myself at His Grace's right hand. I was like a racehorse at the gate, rarin' to go, eager to report for duty at our USO base.

Suddenly, efficiently, the door slid back. And there I stood for one split second, faced with an Honour Guard and General Mark Clark, rows of flapping flags, bugles and trumpets ready to blare greetings to this prestigious party, of which I was in the lead. Until pissed-off secretary firmly pushed me behind the black-suited clerics. I was *not* to be in the newsreels.

* * * * *

I lie outside my tent. Its pungent canvas smell mixes incongruously with the sweetness of flowers planted around the English Officers' Club — their little bit of "sceptred isle." This is my own tent, separate from the other actresses', because my voice is the Allies' answer to the Germans' Axis Sally, and I have to be driven to early-morning broadcasts.

I relish these afternoon sunbaths and watch bomber squadrons fly over from Bari. I am passionately in love with the body of the airplane. I wait for each plane's roar, then peer into the sky as one by one their power sweeps through me in reverberations that last long after they're lost from sight. Lovely vicarious fantasies, and among them the most delightful of all, U.S. bomber pilot, Karl.

Karl, lithe, unpretentious charmer from the corn fields of Nebraska, spells his name unabashedly with a "K," his farming family sufficiently solid in their four generations of American loyalty and shyly proud of their son's military achievements, keep him provided with reams of V-mail and boxes of *Pfeffernuss*, those tasty sugar-coated Christmas cookies.

For Karl, flying is always a celebration. He shares his mother's home-baked cookies with his crew, a talisman to assure them they'll be back in the States by Christmas.

Capri:
The Rest Centre for our unit and for recuperating and over-weary service men and women. Ginny and I are down at the

waterfront eyeing a fishing smack. Its owner introduces himself. Rico. A small ageless man, his clear eyes are shaded by a shapeless cap, his canvas trousers and musty sweater carry the faint but not unpleasant smell of fish. He offers us a leetle *viaggio*, gooood *vino*, *molto pesce*, for leeetle *lira*. Ginny takes over in fluent Italian and begins bargaining. At our backs a cheerful American voice, "We've got money if you don't mind our company," and Karl appears on the scene with his friend, Fred. Delighted, the four of us scramble into the boat. Karl holds out his hand, steadies the boat for me. OK? His touch is firm, gentle, a courtier leading his lady in a pavan. I look up. Karl's eyes are just a shade lighter blue than the Capri sky, his face as open as the Nebraska plains from which he comes. For an instant I see in them what he imagines me to be, an unspoiled girl, the ingenue audiences love. He smiles, the pilot in command, polite, concerned that the fishing smack's owner be accorded the honour due a ship's captain.

Their isn't much to the worn-out pre-war motor, but enough putt-putt to take us languidly around the island. I look at my new Lochinvar. Here is a different sort of airman from those who exude the stereotypical bravura. This gentle youth is unassuming. It's Fred with his navigator's stories who highlights Karl's flying skill and bravery.

Rico feeds us shrimp from a burlap sack. We shell them and feast with olives, bread, and wine. We eat in the boat and Karl, Fred, and I swim from it. The salty Mediterranean tastes as delicious as the shrimp. We catch a glimpse of the Blue Grotto, but Rico warns us away: Danger, *rischio*!

Ginny stays in the boat, fully covered in a gigantic hotel towel to avoid sunburn. Only her lovely blond hair emerges, her enviable blond hair that puts to shame my streaking brown and yellow strands. She signals me to join her. I crawl to the stern.

"Salt water bleaches," she whispers.

Together we bend our heads back into the sea allowing our hair to float behind, two mermaids with but a single thought. Karl watches dazzled while we lie prone, grinning, beguiling Medusas of Capri.

Karl and Fred focus their attention on us. They don't want to talk about their "stuff"; they want to know all about us. Two actresses from New York. Broadway. Wow!

Later, Karl writes me: "I know you didn't expect to hear from me so soon — we were returning from a mission when suddenly I realized that I was in the vicinity of your place. I had Fred check our position and we passed directly over your camp. Because of thick cloud cover and poor visibility, all I had were short glimpses of the ground. But, I tried! I'll be up the next time I draw a test flight. Watch for me now —"

I watch the skies because he flies over frequently and dips his wings to signal hello. He keeps his word. My daily sunbathing takes on tantalizing expectations. I wait for his squadron's flights, aroused by their power above me, thrilled when Karl dips his wings not once but several times. " ... After you left Capri everything seemed to lose its colour.... How is the new play coming along? I'd love to see it, but don't suppose I'll get the chance. Perhaps I'll see you in another at home some day.... I'll try to look you up when I reach New York. Will you save me an hour or two?"

We keep a tight work schedule. We make a big move — Anzio to Rome. A new opening night, this time *The Male Animal.* Magnificent dressing rooms in Mussolini's mistress' theatre, the Eliseo, and I'm waiting for the buzzer to cue me in for my entrance. It's intermission with five minutes to spare. Ginny takes a last drag on her cigarette, Brooke checks her makeup, and Siddy, always the hostess, ushers out the last of our admirers. There's a slight bustling outside our door and Fred, Karl's navigator, pushes past the visitors and apologizes for his late entrance. There are warm, hurried hellos, introductions to Siddy and Brooke, who hadn't met him on Capri.

"And Karl, is he here?" I ask excitedly. "Let's meet after curtain?" The buzzer sounds. Siddy and Brooke murmur their *ciaos* and rush out. I repeat, "Where's Karl?"

"I'm sorry, Sara Lee, Karl won't — Karl went down over … " Fred stands very still, quiet. The buzzer is insistent now. "Your call," Ginny shouts, dashes out. I touch Fred's hand. "*Ciao*," I say, "*ciao*!" and run past him. The applause swells. The curtain's up on the next act.

* * * * *

Flying took on a different meaning. It became routine. We hopped from one place to another until late August, when I made plans to shorten my tour by a few weeks to get back to Broadway for the fall season. A single space was once again found for me, this time on a planeload of airmen flying home. Their tours were finished, too. Once more I was the only woman on the plane. Surrounded by homebound men, I felt comfortable, and took my seat on the aisle next to a pleasant sleepy pilot.

Shades drawn, lights dimmed, the men settle down almost immediately. A few pass a bottle around. Except for the motors' purring, we are wrapped in silence. I fall asleep quickly and dream of my British lover; he is writing a poem to me but it is in Latin. I don't know whether he's saying we will meet again in Cheshire, England, where he was born, or in the Berkshires, Massachussetts, where I am to perform. I urge him to speak. His lips move yet he is mute. I awaken. My restless head has sagged on my fellow passenger's shoulder. I sit up with a start, rearrange my uniform and groggily look around. Nobody stirs. I'm left alone with my waking dreams.

The drawn shade is buckled just enough to allow a flicker of light against the sealed window on my right. Quietly I reach over my sleeping seat-mate. I want to lift that shade. I know we've been airborne too long to catch a glimpse of the Italy I will never forget, but still I want to look into the blackness, search for a farewell hint. I peer into the night. To my surprise, the propellers are giving off little bursts of

Fourth of July sparklers. It's very pretty but also very strange. I've never seen fireworks like this during night flights. Gently I nudge my companion, point to the window, ask, Is that OK? He barely opens his eyes, mutters OK, and closes his eyes. I can't take mine off the sparklers, which are getting brighter and brighter. I shake the airman's arm again, Something is wrong. Please. Look out there. He sits bolt upright, conditioned to respond to tense warnings, glances sharply out the window, climbs over me and darts up the aisle to the captain's cabin. There's a soundless alert among the sleeping bodies, a ripple of movement. Almost cavalierly the co-pilot appears. "We're turning back."

It seems as if each man wordlessly accepts the rerouting, holds the plane's control in his own hands, determined that nothing will bring us down, nothing prevent our getting home.

Back in the Azores, we are told to bed down in the barracks for the night, told how lucky we are. "You almost reached the point of no return!"

Long before dawn, cold and in shock, I am told the engine has been repaired. We are ordered back onto the same plane. I go. I never utter a peep, shiver my timbers, or break into tears.

I've flown thousands of miles over the North American continent and Europe since the war, in varying states of joy, horror, alcoholic or valiumed daze. The need to survive, to taste every moment left to me, is encouragement enough now to say without the slightest embarrassment, No thank you, I won't fly. Not now. Not for a while, anyway.

The Strip

HE IS AT THE BOTTOM OF THE POOL, his hair floating like silver octopus suckers in chlorinated blue. Why does he not rise? I am waiting. I peer into the deep water waiting for him to rise. I want to photograph him, force his eyes open, see him close up; he is so blurred. He is at the bottom and I am not there. But I am there at his hospital bed, looking at my colossus. His giant feet and hands are uncovered, the sheet drawn down for relief from the Hollywood heat, his eyes still closed. The graph above him moves steadily, his heart thumps a dull tattoo, his brain is dead.

Apollo, stand at the gates of Rhodes with me; come back to Greece with our children and save our world, Protector of the Muses.

I will forget you, force my memory to fail. I am here. You are not. A heart too big, a brain befuddled, now dead.

I miss him, but I do not want him back. I love him, but let him go.

* * * * *

It's unreal to me; like a soap opera.

1945: I am in Las Vegas to get a divorce. Then I'm going on to Hollywood for a screen test at Warner Bros. But en route I trip over an old woman's feet at the Hotel Last Frontier's pool. We exchange apologies. We laugh. She offers me her clinking pitcher of iced gin and tonic. She's bubbling.

"I'm up for the weekend from L.A. My son Dick lives here in Vegas. He's the architect for the hotel's new additions. He'll be joining me anytime now. We always have a drink or two before sundown."

I eye the pitcher already half-empty, sundown nowhere on the horizon.

"And where do you come from? NEW YORK! Just finished a Broadway play! You must meet my son."

And so I do.

He's a handsome man, tall, broad-shouldered, with dazzling blue eyes that slant intriguingly when he smiles. And that is often. His voice is mellow, inviting. And his sleek salt-and-pepper hair contrasts surprisingly with a youthful impression. I like him.

He takes us to dinner. He and I dance. He says he'd settled in Vegas several years ago after his divorce. He marvels at my rhythm, I at his fancy footwork.

Sixteen years my senior, he tells me.

We walk his mother to her room, he escorts me to mine. We fall in love.

And so we marry.

* * * * *

Family had been a sometime thing for me. Each production and every play formed a new family that dissolved at the end of the run.

I, Sara Lee Harris, actor, began to create a new family, a permanent one: New York, my apartment, Broadway, became memories. Dick was a local celebrity, a catch for restless grass widows, until I came along footloose from Broadway, a gatecrasher whose background puzzled the curious. (Is Richard Ryerson Stadelman's new wife a chorus girl, an actress? What does that *mean*, she's from the legitimate theatre?)

The fact that our marriage was a second for both of us caused not a ripple. Even then repeat offenders in Vegas shared big business with divorce and the roulette wheel (one friend's primly devout mother kept the busiest wedding chapel in town).

Adoption, on the other hand, was an event. Our friends were enthusiastic, but my pious Catholic next-door neighbour made it her calling to tell the curious, in confidence of course, that we had adopted because I wanted to keep my size-seven figure.

Kris came to us aged seven days. He was long-legged, sweet-tempered. Cathy was still to come.

* * * * *

Oh, Isaac Bashevis Singer, who ever would have thought your demons and angels are real ghosts who mischievously peep out from behind half-closed doors to stir things up fifty years after a done deed?

The phone rang one day. Our Mormon friend, Dr. Woodbury, told us he had an unusual case. A couple had come to him for an abortion, which he wouldn't perform.

"Would you be willing to support a woman during the remaining months of her pregnancy? She's a good person," he said, "out-of-state, a pitiful situation. The baby's father's a small-time gambler, married, large family to support. He wants to disentangle from her ... "

It was a late pregnancy. The mother was indecisive about carrying the child and the conflict was seriously undermining her health. She needed special care and medication.

"With supervised treatment she'll deliver successfully. Would you and Dick think about it and pray over it?"

His question was an answer to prayers already offered.

We supported the mother and waited the months for Cathy to be born. She was premature. But when she came to us from the incubator, smaller than the palm of Dick's hand, she was perfect, beautiful, without scar or blemish.

For Kris, now two, this tiny baby was more than a puzzle: should he take the squirming thing, hold it, kiss it like Mommy did? Uhuh. His brown velvet eyes peered into her half-opened blue ones. "Cathy," I murmured. "Caffey," he said, touched her and frowned. "Your sister," I said, patting his wheat-coloured hair. Kris whispered, seriously, "*My* Caffey!"

The legal year for adoption finalization was about to end when we received an order to appear before Judge MacNamee.

We sat in his office, he behind his desk, I directly in front of it with Dick beside me, facing "the petitioner," my daughter's biological father.

If I ever knew the petitioner's name, I do not remember it now. Blanked it out. He was muscular, broad-shouldered, squat. From the beginning of the interview he leaned forward, his hands clasped in his lap as if the matter were settled and he was simply waiting patiently for the roulette wheel to stop at the number of his bet.

Dick sat tall, still, against the back of his chair; only his nervous fingers were tapping. I was motionless, frozen.

"Well, sir," asked the judge, "what exactly do you want?"

"Like I wrote you," the petitioner began, "I have my divorce now," and added truculently, "married the mother of my child — "

"*Your* child — " I interrupted. The judge softly reprimanded me.

The man was unctuous. "I know how awful this must be for you and Mr. Stadelman, but we're ready now to take on the baby."

Judge MacNamee looked down at the documents on his desk, carefully turned several pages. "This couple longed for this baby so much," he said. "They supported it for months before its birth, waited to bring it home from the incubator and have been its mother and father for over a year, and now you are ready to reclaim this child?"

"Your Honour, I know you're a Roman Catholic man so you can understand the fix we were in. See, my ... my wife ... is the daughter of a minister and she couldn't tell her family our ... my ... situation."

Judge MacNamee was abrupt. "Isn't it true that you cornered every doctor in Vegas begging for an abortion?"

Silence. The man unclasped his hands, wiped them on his trousers. "Yes." He half-turned his bulk toward my husband, looking for man-to-man-of-the-world support. "You know how it is." His watery blue eyes appealed to mutually remembered youthful pranks. But Dick sat firm, his eyes never flickering, his hands clenched. Not a word.

The judge rose. "Give me some time to study this case," he said, and led the man to the door. When he closed it I broke into sobs. A sliver of tear slid down Dick's face. As the judge walked us to the door, he put his hands gently on our shoulders. "I'll let you know in a few weeks."

We trusted a few close friends to pray with us every day for those weeks, trying to hide our anxiety from our children. But tensions between Dick and me became intolerable. There were vast overtime expenses because of alterations to his design for Bugsy Siegel's Hotel Flamingo. Mr. Murder-Incorporated-Bugsy's mistress, Virginia Hill, was running the show, and running it from Bugsy's bed, where Dick was called one afternoon to a meeting, and found the two of them in it, wearing nothing but Dick's blueprints. The building's budget was ballooning. Dick insisted the full terms of his contract be met, and instituted a suit to collect it.

Our nerves were frayed; abrupt anonymous phone calls: "Drop it!" Did this mean the lawsuit or the adoption? Two men shadowed us wherever we turned. We barred our windows, double-locked the doors, picnicked only in our own backyard, avoided outdoor jaunts. And waited.

We prayed deeply and shaped our lives around the hope, the conviction that "every good gift and every perfect gift" would be realized.

Cathy was awarded to us. At the same time Bugsy decided to settle out of court with Richard Ryerson Stadelman and Associates.

Bugsy shook hands with Dick! "I hear you've been bothered with phone calls. I'll look into that, maybe I can help. And I hope my two boys looked after you OK? Didn't make a nuisance? Oh! And Dick? *Mazel tov* on the new baby!"

* * * * *

I was asked to produce a pageant inaugurating the new Elks Stadium in Vegas. My smashing musical play (slightly reminiscent of *Oklahoma!*, I admit) was proudly embraced as a cultural event. The respectable matrons began to accept me.

I found a role to play and honed my persona to fit it. I became a zealous church worker, organized readings for children at Las Vegas' one-room library, and broadcast fundraisers for the Red Cross on Radio KENO.

* * * * *

I wake up thirsty and go to the kitchen for a glass of water. The house is dark, except for a single lamp above Dick's drawing board in the study. He hasn't heard me, so I pad barefoot to look over his shoulder. His clean blunt fingers, that move deftly at the board, that tap the steering wheel when he's driving, that nervously tap his nose when he's thinking, are completely relaxed. On his board are wonderful fantasies: rounded turrets, swirling arches and steep inclines, leading to gardens melting into a vast sea. In the lower right-hand corner he's block-lettered MILNER'S OFFICE BUILDING. Dick has abstracted the famous abbey of Mont St. Michel from memory of our one brief stay there, and is dreaming of transposing it to the corner of Fifth and Church Streets in Las Vegas, Nevada.

I tiptoe back to bed, my imagination at rest with his, my sleepy prayers a niggling wish that I, too, could give definite form to some Mont St. Michel of my own.

* * * * *

Dick persuaded the Hotel Last Frontier to place an historic (1905 — historic for Vegas) building on the quaint Western Village he was designing for them. It was an old warehouse from which goods had been shipped out by mule. But when Dick was through refurbishing and remodelling it, in 1948, we called it the Bird Cage Theatre, Nevada's first professional Equity company. I made it Open Sesame for myself. I was actor, producer, and woman about town.

The stars I hired, men and women leads and supporting roles, were a mixed bag of fruit, coming as they did from Hollywood. Zazu Pitts — It is *Zay-zoo*, she imperiously pronounced — played in *The Late Christopher Bean*; Edward Everett Horton did his perennial *Springtime for Henry*.

They were so big in their day when TV didn't reach our desert homes and movies were the thing. Their star temperaments (*Zay-zoo* demanded a fresh box of chocolate turtles each night on her dressing room table) and their immense salaries went through our budget like butter through an English muffin. Still, because of my more recent Broadway credits, I was the one who rang up the jackpot at the box office starring in *Joan of Lorraine* (Maxwell Anderson)— "Better than Ingrid Bergman's version in New York" was the buzz — *The Heiress* (Ruth and Augustus Goetz), *The Glass Menagerie* (Tennessee Williams), and several lesser Broadway comedy leftovers.

All this demanded more emotional energy than I was able to handle. I frequently exploded in outbursts of rage, and always felt guilty. I was like a juggler trying to keep a half-dozen knives in the air, cutting myself on one after another. In retrospect I see this pipsqueak producer with her make-believe authority interviewing, auditioning, throwing her one hundred pounds around. It was fun! Of course pipsqueak has two meanings: an insignificant twerp, or, for the more linguistically sophisticated, a small high-velocity shell (German, W.W.I). At the Bird Cage, as around town, my appearance was the former, my nature the latter. More than occasionally I went off in the wrong places and the wrong directions. A little dalliance because your husband is preoccupied and a guy looks interesting, then a little guilt followed by an explosion.

A little psychiatrist kept me at the required distance while I sobbed my repeated question, Why can't I hold everything together, career, family, and, yes, the predicted potential stardom? Why can't I manage my life à la Ingrid Bergman? Why does my public façade have to fall apart?

Dr. W. had no answer, although he kindly invited our family to join his for Hanukkah celebrations.

In short order my psychiatrist was run out of town because of huge gambling debts and yes, yes, yes, Ingrid ran away with Rosselini.

Then, after three too-exciting seasons, the Bird Cage closed without a tweet and faith became my escape from that humiliation.

I dove into religion, but faith was a deeper pool than I'd imagined. We always taught our children to pray and now we made it a regimen, determined that the children's first response to every situation should be prayer.

Church activities became intense. My social circle revolved like a whirling dervish around brightly smiling hausfraus. They seemed happy. I wanted to be happy! I wanted to qualify for membership in their domestic sorority. If I no longer had a theatre for my talents, there was always the kitchen.

Curtain up. Act II.

Scene: I am a bouffant-skirted decorously-aproned lady. I give my maid an unexpected holiday. Now I, too, am a neighbourhood homemaker, chef, and earth mother. Impatient with Betty Crocker, I improvise. Hadn't I been an inventive improviser at The Neighborhood Playhouse? (How long and long ago it seems!) Well then, in with the stuffing, the turkey, yams, apple pie, pecan tarts, spices, garnishes, and a non-alcoholic punch. As the newly appointed Sunday School Supervisor, I have to be a role model. I whistle while I work.

My perfect last-minute touch will be cranberry sauce *extraordinaire*, not from a can, but from boiled berries augmented with walnuts, raisins, orange peel, and set to cool in my crystal bowl. I've suffered the local ladies' daily dusting of their family treasures; this crystal bowl is the only one I can lay claim to. With a little effort I sometimes manage to squeeze a few tears from my eyes when friends drop in for tea and I show them dear old grandmother's inheritance so thoughtfully donated to me. So sweet, so considerate of my family, who declined the treasure, especially as I'd never met dear old grandmother, who was dead decades before I was born.

Everything is *parfait*. My three-year-old daughter's eyes tell me so as we hum together, "Jesus loves me this I know for the Bible tells me so." Cathy, pigtailed and freckle-faced, drags the kitchen ladder to the kitchen counter, climbs its three steps the better to behold the wonder of crystal and cranberries.

I decide I must put away my pride and originality with it. This *pièce de résistance* calls for Betty Crocker's steady hand. As I reach for the cookbook, Cathy reaches for the bowl. There is a crash! I whip around to see crystal shards, nuts and assorted fruits spread on the floor. I shriek, "WHAT HAVE YOU DONE!"

Cathy stands on the ladder, frozen, terrified. She closes her eyes and murmurs, " ... Fatherwhoartinheavenhallowedbethy name ... "

My world stops turning. I rip off my apron, drop the basting ladle and smother my three-year-old with kisses.

I don't need to read Jung to see the symbols in the shards. I need a change of scene. I am played out trying to keep up with my sorority sisters in the domestic prelature. From every window I look, there is desert.

* * * * *

A storm was brewing out there. National outbursts of political suspicion were fanning my personal panic. Whispering innuendoes hung like heavy black clouds over anyone previously associated with actors, artists, professionals considered upper- or lower-case liberals. Were you, have you ever been, have you ever known: communists, socialists, anarchists, leftists, trade union activists? Nevada's powerful Senator McCarren made sure that Las Vegas would appear lily-white and my smiling church friends excelled as patriots. Efficient housekeepers with prying eyes, they allowed for no deviation from cleanliness and godliness. Every nook and corner must be sealed against the Reds' dust.

I needed to houseclean, too. I remembered crates of books that had never been unpacked, a legacy from my first husband, honoured scholar, medalled paratrooper, blacklisted, his career and reputation burned to a crisp along with his friends'. Some of them were prominent; some even on the cover of *Time*. Would rumours seep through the water-tight sands and reach me? I hadn't read his books but I had them.

Dick and I had bought a fine piece of desert property beyond The Strip. We named it Dunesand. Early mornings, evenings at dusk, over weekends, we'd jeep across back-breaking mounds of sand and dream up our house-to-be. Now in this treasured oasis I determined to burn my past.

I didn't see any irony in the fact that just a few years ago I'd entertained our troops in a war against book-burners and idea-scorching replicas of Torquemada who were supposed to have prepared the world for a new age of peace and tranquility. I wanted a fire at Dunesand. I pleaded with Dick to help me rip apart bindings, tear out pages by the hundreds, thousands.

"Why?" asked Dick, western, easy-going, politically indifferent, socially safe. "Why?"

"Just strike the match!" I screamed. "Help me!"

Betrayal came easily. I watched ten years of my first husband's special library, Marx, Engels, Lenin, Stalin, all their theories to unite the workers of the world for the promised land savagely licked black in my bonfire. The books burned, every one of them, two huge crates-full. I only kept a blue leather-bound King James Bible, a childhood gift that I'd forgotten was in with the others.

We never put Dunesand to any other use.
Sold it.

* * * * *

In the middle of the night my asthma attack begins. I sit up reading, gasping, choking until it's no longer possible to stay in bed.

The children must not hear my agony as I struggle to breathe. I must not awaken my husband again, not be driven another time to the hospital where an injection will put me to sleep, but not cure me. There will be a next attack. This time I'm sure I can't make it, I'm dying. I gasp, crawl, stretch my whole body toward the door, toward that open space where the still scalding summer air might help me to breathe. I reach the door, pull myself up by the doorknob, twist, turn it as quietly as possible and stumble into the stifling desert, dig into my pyjama pocket for the car keys, writhe, turn on the ignition and go, go along the blue-black highway.

No speed limits here. I whip faster and faster, the breeze starts up. Air. I race to Mount Charleston, past the darkened ranch homes. Oh God, thank you, I'm breathing. The stranglehold across my chest is lifting. I swerve left, take the single-lane highway, swing into the climb up that wonderful mountain with its promised freedom. Oxygen waits for me. I lean into each dangerous curve, exultant, sure of sleep once I reach the peak, familiar to me from our summer-evening picnics. My windows are wide open when I reach the lookout, breathe deeply and hear myself whispering Oh, lovely, air ... lovely. Stillness. Sleep.

There are humming sounds and little beams of light like flashing bugs. Am I dreaming? I open my eyes slowly. There are cars parked near mine. It is still very dark, the thick darkness that comes just before dawn. People are chattering quietly, moving carefully as if preparing for something. At this hour?

I sit up, peer out the window I'd had to close part-way against the cold mountain air. I draw the car blanket more tightly around me.

A friendly woman's voice says, "Hi!" and adds, "Isn't it exciting, waiting?"

Waiting for what, I think, but don't dare ask. Instead I murmur, "Awfully cold though, isn't it."

She laughs. "Once the test happens it'll be hot as hell. Something to tell our kids about!"

The test! Of course! The nuclear test scheduled for dawn. The local press has been heralding it. Feeling chipper now, I jump out of the car.

A male voice is giving polite but definite instructions: it is time to synchronize watches, close windows, close eyes, put our heads down, way down into the car seats when he gives the signal.

"NOW! DUCK!"

Head buried in the plush seat of my Cadillac, I hear a whooshing as if a storm is about to burst, and with the whooshing I SEE, see the car's innards stripped in X-rayed light.

"It's safe now!" a man's voice calls.

We scramble from our cars and stand together. There's cheering, hand-shaking, celebration.

Someone yells, "We've made it! We've fucked the Reds!"

Laughter, bottles clicking. There's an afterglow in the desert below. I turn my back, look at the other desert from which I came, still sombre, sleeping.

Doors slam. Slowly the cars start down the mountain.

I am the last to follow.

THE STRIPPING

I go down the mountain. It's steep but the brakes are in good shape. Not like that terrible night last year when I relieved Richard at the wheel driving the one-lane pitch-black highway to Los Angeles. Glorious, unlimited Nevada speed laws. Richard and I in our open convertible sing one hymn after another, the whistling wind an obbligato to this weekend's freedom while the children are safely settled back home with our housekeeper, Alice, in Las Vegas. We always carry the Bible with us and read passages aloud. This time the hymn-singing seems to follow our quiet meditations.

Like a demon, like a devil out of hell, a fierce beam shoots from an oncoming car. There is no escape from its blinding. I swerve, see the deep ditch to my right, put my foot on the brake. My instinct flashes, Don't lock the brakes! We come to a grinding, jarring halt, tipped almost on our side but not turned over. We look at each other, at the hollow desert darkness, and in unison say, God, thank you.

I rest my head on the steering wheel, Richard puts his against the dashboard. At exactly the same instant we see what saved the wheels from locking. Our Bible has fallen under the brake pedal.

So hard to pierce the veil now, almost thirty years after his death. The tales of his childhood in Kearney, Nebraska: the family thriving on the rich things of life, especially whiskey and mother Mary Genevieve's great baking; his father the first to drive an automobile (I think a Studebaker), and Richard the first of three children to be dandled, made much of with his first spoken request for "wicky and punkin pie!"

When they moved to Bakersfield, California, Dick's father continued investing in grandiose speculations until the Depression. Mr. Stadelman Sr. gloried in being an entrepreneur, had bigger dreams and bigger debts, friends who wouldn't or couldn't repay loans, and one day he put a pistol to his head. The police told Dick where his father was, and left it to him to pull his father's bloody body from the locked car.

Dick remained haunted by failure throughout his life despite his achievements. And he never forgot the charm of whiskey, even while watching his fragile demure mother

Mary Genevieve totter sweetly through the years, distilled in it, her adored husband's legacy.

* * * * *

There are all kinds of titillating Gospel stories. Accidents can melt into coincidences when people break Bread together. Anecdotes exchanged turn water into Blood, winding sheets wring out miracles. Hearts break egg-shell thin, yolking one story to another.

Yes! I love to tell the story, seventy times seven: desert fahrenheit, one swimming pool, three children, no pear tree, sage-brush only, and me.

Maude phoned: "Ya know," she said, in that honey-suckled Memphis drawl, "if ya can't take the heat — "

"Damn it honey-chile, I'm not *in* the kitchen."

"Oooo, what you said," she giggled, and we both remembered our upright, uptight ladies at church.

"I've been outside watching the children having one hell — heck-of-a — of a time with their favourite playmate little Jimmy from across the way. Just came in for a second's air-cooled relief to answer your magnolia-sweet call." The phone slithered from my sweaty hand. "I'm dying by deeegrees."

"Now Sara," Maude crooned in her more serious voice, "a good Christian Scientist must hold to the truth. Mary Baker Eddy tells us that we live, move, and have our being in God our infinite life, so," resuming her Southern birthright, "ya can't be dyin'!" And serious again, "Isn't that swimming pool finished *yet*?"

"No, Maude angel, the cement is still not dry enough to fill it, should be in a day or two, Dick says, but on the hottest day of the year *the* pool is one concrete waterless hole!"

Cries of Mommy, Mommy! cut into the phone call. These are not the usual brother and sister howls, the seven-year-old brother's complaints against his five-year-old sister. These are screeches in unison. Mommy! Mommy!

Two terrified faces appear at the sliding glass door. Kris' and Cathy's hands press against it and pound it. Hurry Mommy, hurry! they scream. I race to them, look in the direction they're pointing. Their playmate Jimmy lies curled like a bleeding fetus on the blue stucco at the deep end of our empty swimming pool.

We rush to him, but there are no steps down the ten-foot drop. God, God, dear God I cry, and fly to the shallow end, the children trailing. My sandals fall off. The children race around them. I jump down, run to Jimmy, take him in my arms and carry his limp little body to the pool's edge. His eyelids flutter, blood trickles into them from his forehead.

Jimmy, I whisper. There is a tiny moan, then a sob. My children and I look at each other. Lord, Lord, I call, help us, help us. And then we say the first words that come so naturally to us: Our Father who art in heaven, hallowed be thy name. Jimmy darling, do you hear me, try to pray with us. Only a word I beg. (He's a Catholic, my mind keeps interrupting. But even Catholics must know the Lord's Prayer!) I hold him closer, quietly Cathy and Kris join me, Hallowed be thy name. Jimmy haltingly murmurs Kingdom, and we say Thy will be done as I gently rock him. He adds another word, a phrase, the tears pour down his freckled face. He sits up shaking but alert. I carry him a few paces but tough little Jimmy wriggles down.

Hand-in-hand the four of us walk slowly across the street to face his mother. I knock. She answers the door smiling, hugely pregnant, one crawling child clinging to her starched skirt. She's so surprised to see a friendly Protestant neighbour she doesn't notice Jimmy — none of us on our street has ever visited her before. I say, O Mrs. — and can't remember her name, if I ever knew it.

Startled, she asks, Has Jimmy misbehaved? I tell her what has happened. Jimmy bursts into tears. She strokes his hair, touches his scratched face and arms. I ask, Is there anything — should we take Jimmy to the hospital? (I, Christian

Scientist, offer to pay for a doctor, X-rays.) — Are you *sure* there's nothing?

Jimmy's mother holds him close. Don't worry, she says, We're all OK. You're trembling, she says to me. Come on in, sit down, we'll have a cup of tea.

I stand at the door in awe, "We all said The Lord's Prayer ... together. *All* of us."

But I didn't go in.

One Encore After Another

ONE DIDN'T HAVE TEA WITH CATHOLICS. One did have drinks with them at a bar. For business reasons.

My forays into Catholic circles were met with calculated coolness by priests and business acquaintances. They were polite in that charming Irish way: coquetry spread on servility. My husband needed their architectural commissions as much as they needed his unquestioned technical experience. That made for great barbecue exchanges among the men but left me with their women. Unlike my Protestant friends, these wives were not eager to talk religion. In the late forties, early fifties, everyone was eager to appear a "normal" American.

"My Kevin was a changed man when he came back from the war, but he's normal now." (That's what you think, but I bet that Madam Lazonga down Route Sixty-six ...)

"I know just what you mean, Mary." (Like hell you do. Or maybe you do?)

"Well girls, like I always say, 'Keep the home fires burning.'" (Big laugh, some giggles.)

I called a halt before recipe exchanges began: "You know, when I was in Italy I was so impressed with the Catholic churches. In Siena, there was this one with a beautiful fresco of St. Catherine — "

No takers.

"I mean she was really something, trying to get your Pope back from Avignon — "

"Our Pope's in Rome, dear."

"You're thinking of St. Catherine of the Wheel, the one who was beheaded," Lucy smiles.

I'm about to explain what I found out during my time in Siena, but steely-eyed Mary cuts in, "Oooo, girls, the boys are calling us, steaks are ready!"

I want answers. Big question: How can your corrupt church, which I've been taught is the Biblical whore of Babylon, produce such great art, those inspired cathedrals, murals, and sculptures? How did that all happen?

Better to leave sleeping bitches lie. One doesn't discuss religion or politics in company, Mother taught me.

Sink your teeth into that beef!

Meantime, I stayed with the Calvinist church of my childhood. Unhappily. It exacerbated my conflict by tying me tighter to surroundings that were dry, lacking the juice I needed to assert or to be myself. The Bird Cage (preceded by the stadium splash, *Vegas in Calico*) had been popular theatre, but didn't satisfy my craving for beauty. Sure Catholics had their bourgeoisie, too, and I didn't want any more of their cookouts either. But the Church's art made her more than attractive to my hungry tastes. Restlessness was stalking me again.

* * * * *

Like puffballs from our cottonwood trees, that restlessness blows me across continents back to my old stomping grounds — Columbia University and environs. "A change'll do you good," Dick says. Does he mean it'll do him good as well? I know, and think he does, too, that his work in Vegas has come to a dead end. His partners are betraying him, siphoning off his clients and his creative ideas. He has been through betrayal before, with his first wife. Does he sense that his second wife is also betraying him? I don't know. We will never face this between us.

I'll have no shortage of funds for tuition this time, for dorm residence, airfares. I become a cross-country wife and mother flying the New York-Las Vegas route, alternating weekends with my husband and children. Now you see me now you don't.

This is victory! This is not the Depression-era nightmare of my teenage years when I'd had to work part-time to keep a scholarship afloat, hoard nickels for long subway rides from Brooklyn to Manhattan, furiously smoke cigarettes to stave off hunger. (My suave French professor had daily warned me in the courtyard, *Mademoiselle, vous fumez trop*. At home my mother had smelled smoke from my room: "Oh God!" came up from the downstairs landing, "Oh God, my heart!

That's what bad girls do, Saralee. Oh my heart, my heart!" (She spent three days in bed.)

I'd been saved from collapse in those days by a circle of persistent endearing radical friends: great talk, great books, great people — first Socialists then Communists. The former, unlike my family, were intellectual, rational, remote, but, like my family, were too argumentative. The latter were affectionate and attractive. One of the most brilliant chose me for his bed and bride. We lost our virginity together and promised to love forever. I believed I'd become a woman. (What a crock!) Marriage seemed as good a way to leave Brooklyn as commuting by subway.

Jay was an idealist, one who acted upon his convictions. When the United States entered W.W.II he joined up, eager to become a pilot. He was considered unsuitable pilot material. (We learned from a fighter pilot neighbour that intellectual Jews "question orders too much, you know?") Instead Jay was trained as a paratrooper and shipped to the Pacific. Obviously he never questioned the order to jump, and won both appropriate medals and promotions.

But before the war there is a scene in front of Dean Murray Butler's house. We are demanding that Columbia lift its racism and colour quotas. We of the Young Communist League (the girls in lisle stockings, chanting "Stop silk imports from Japan!") demand sanctions against Germany. We are the "premature anti-fascists." (The FBI frightened my patriotic mother a few years later when they vetted me before I went overseas with the USO.)

Jay and I take our turn at midnight, alone except for the two policemen patrolling on horseback. To the rhythm of their horses' clop, clop, clop, clop, Jay, remembering his parents' tales of long-ago Slovakia, whispers, "Cossacks, Cossacks." And I whisper boldly in unison with him, "Cossacks!"

SCENE:
Dean Alexander's office at Columbia's New College (Teachers' College). I have teaching potential. Despite fluctuating grades I am to have free tuition to finish my Master's — with study in Europe, too! One condition. Dissociate now from left-wing friends.

I can't. Won't.

(A short time later Dean Alexander was fired from New College when his Nazi affiliation was uncovered.)

* * * * *

In New York at Columbia the second time around, this once-again liberated woman plunges into playwriting courses and discovers that she no longer wants to speak other people's words, but her own.

She wants to study, to think, to *learn* to think. There can be no going back to Las Vegas. She and her husband decide to explore art together — and separately. He will study with Frank Lloyd Wright in Arizona. She'll go to Yale, experiment with playwriting, find out how to form her own words to speak. The children will stay with her and they'll all join forces again in the spring when Frank Lloyd Wright's Taliesin moves to its summer home in Wisconsin.

There is so much unfinished business, but how can she finish what she still doesn't understand? She only knows that she must broaden her perspectives. She doesn't know that her return to Columbia has brought her back so close to the Jesus upon whose lap she'd sat in the window, back to within reach of that Sanctuary Lamp little Irene had told her signified that Jesus was really present in her church. She doesn't know that that lamp in the bosom of "The Whore" was capable of flickering its way to Yale, New Haven, or any haven, and take back someone who thought she was moving forward.

Deepwood

Drum beats and rattles ...

New Haven, Deepwood Drive and The-House-*The-Bridge*-Built. It was beautiful, it was maddening, it was terrible. It was Thornton and Isabel Wilder's home — up a steep hill, dark brown, unassuming, nestled, almost hidden in the woods.

The author of *The Bridge of San Luis Rey* enthusiastically used its royalties to buy the property. His devoted sister kept it and him in order.

I will have to go back
not old enough
to be frightened
not young enough
to be free
the children away
to be captured
for weekends.

For the months I studied at Yale that house became our home. The children loved it. They dashed for the back garden shuffling the crackling autumn leaves, taking delight tossing them at each other. This was a new experience away from our desert home of sage and cacti. I saw them through the open French doors while I browsed through my course notes or wrote to my husband in Arizona.

This is their garden I thought. Mine is a different garden, brambled, bitter, burning ...

I go
to the top
of the staircase
at night
in my nightgown
wondering looking

for someone
to enter that door
below in the woods.
But who?
a lawyer perhaps
a friend of the Wilders
young enough for gossip
old enough to collect
the rent.
How did it happen
the rosary, the phone
and the priest?

YALE:

The priest was at the bottom of a spiral staircase. I was at the top. He was surrounded by a circle of arguing, questioning, challenging students. He was calm among the curious.

I furious
like a sabre
cut through
the throng
to the priest

"I want to speak to you. I must speak to you." (Won't take no for an answer. He must come now, now, now. I must speak. He must listen.)

All sound ceases except his voice. The Drama Department's Green Room absorbs the young men and women as they melt away into its shadows. Rude, crude, I stand demanding. The little dog-collared priest's blue eyes twinkle.

"If you don't mind joining me for lunch at the corner drugstore, we can talk there." Not so much a question as a polite invitation to a drama student who he thinks will never refuse a free meal. But this is different. I know I'll pay.

It's Friday. In the drugstore we find a table. We sit. I'm against the wall. He orders a tuna sandwich (Catholics and their meatless Fridays!). I order corned beef on rye.

> In desperation only
> I seek the mysterious
> clutch the straw
> or the anchor
> when drowning
> go down either way.

I cannot remember how it happened. Did I say I wanted to become a Catholic? Hardly. That I wanted to learn about the Catholic religion? Doubt it. How did it begin? Tell me about yourself? No. First thing he ordered that tuna sandwich.

"Why are you interested in the Catholic Church?"

"I don't know ... " — long pause — "I think it's because of St. Catherine of Siena. I saw Andrea Vanni's portrait of her when our armies were stopped just outside of Bologna."

His blue eyes twinkled again. "She's a Dominican."

"What's that?" I asked.

"A religious order within the church. I'm one of them. In fact that's my name, Dominic."

And that's how it happened, out of desperation, out of loneliness, confusion, depression, insomnia.

Series of montages, superimposures: We walk, he, even then, with small faltering footsteps. In fact he was small. Dominic Thomas Rover seemed quite timid in class but articulate and wonderfully witty when we spoke together. He gave me my first real rosary and I think he was surprised that I knew the litany.

> What way? What way?
> the way of the little girl
> going to church

O Rose of Lima
who is she?

I told Father Rover of my little Catholic friend Irene and her family the Wings, all Catholic but the father.

I go hand in hand
with freckled Irene
and her dangling rosary
my mother's amber beads
taken surreptitiously
for roped attachment.
Irene goes into the confessional —
secret space —
I sit grasping those beads
stare at the red lighted lamp
later learn its name:
Sanctuary.
Did you know people
see things there
visions?

I told Father:

Irene's mom. Always dressed in black, rocks back and forth on her front porch, not enclosed like ours ... her rosary beads black, too ... back and forth she answers a few of my precocious questions and always with the same answer:

"Mysteries."

"What is the Holy Ghost?"

"Mystery."

Mrs. Wing smoothes chocolate over whole wheat bread — only one slice. She bakes it. My mother can't. (But she cants.)

Irene's mother's skirts are long, aproned; my mother's short — good legs revealed.

In their dining room, too, Mrs. Wing rocks, reading Louisa M. Alcott. Why?

"Is Alcott Catholic?"

"Mystery."

Her hair is long, a bun in back; my mother's bobbed short (with sobs — done secretly), a shocking step forward.

Irene's mother hangs out the laundry (no maid — NO MAID!). Irene's mother is old Mrs. Wing. (Mr. Wing's part Indian they say.)

Did we ever know
another Wing
a name like that
a word like that?
He walks down
the street neat
each day
dignified straight
an arrow winging where?
He's clean
unlike ritually clean
grandfather
also tall but blue-eyed
with yarmulke and hatred
handsome cruel
he pees in the street
pees on the goyim.

Mary was a whore
he says
pork causes boils
terrific trayfic
traffic
asks me to teach him
to write his name
for money I do
cursively
no shame yet

memory wiped out
in the snow ...

I think it was Updike who said that shame has the taste of authenticity since *La Chute*, since Adam and Eve.

In the snow
in the alley
beside Irene's house
we sit on the sled
and pee into our gloves
a victory of pee.
If only I could wee
like a boy
try turning backwards
on the toilet seat.

Seated in the classroom at Yale, D.H. Lawrence grabs me ... *The Princess* ... I adapt her into a one-acter. Can't get permission from his notorious famous German wife to mount it.

I am a princess
with Cadillac to mount —
not yet Catholic —
that's another class
where passion directs me
to Francis of Assisi
and I write a play
without balls.
No good comes
from Nazareth.

How could it?

Go on searching
one orgasm after another

with that Spaniard
researching monkeys' brains
knocking on doors
searching knocking
watching the submarine
in sub-zero weather
spear the ice
his huge erection
proudly emerging
from the bathtub
O!
macho machismo
calling out her name
some Japanese beauty
he wants can't
forget her cunt
he's Catholic
big big C
O hell
what's the difference
romance
with instruction
in, of course,
the Catholic faith
from another priest
a fucking-priest
who invites me
to dinner steaks
you see he prepares
the feast and while
the potatoes bake
lurches for me
in the living room
this can't be
no, not a priest!
I leave in a hurry

a virgin like Mary
I know my rosary
don't forget.

This history will be viewed, of course, as I see it now — quite inaccurately regarding sequences of events interpreted from a distant perspective of forty years. If the history is revisionist, it's not intentional. So many things aroused my curiosity. So many things frightened me.

The many bedrooms in The-House-*The-Bridge*-Built.

There was my bedroom with the phone beside me on the night table. I used that phone to make desperate night calls to Father Rover, clinging to the rosary, not as a talisman but for deep prayer that finally led to meditative peace, and sometimes sleep.

And the Cadillac. A beige Cadillac was just fine for speeding along to the children at their boarding school, but asinine for driving to class and the library at Yale.

In retrospect, that is as embarrassing as the Spanish doctor. (I can't remember how I met that bastard but his being a cousin of the playwright Lorca was a great attraction.)

Can we go forward
without going back?

A good Catholic
gives me her fudge
recipe,
invites me to share
sex
I say no,
thank you
think yuk.

How far back to go?
Brooklyn

not much there
anymore
other Catholics,
of course.

What distinguishes
the lower middle class
from the upper distingués?
Across the street
a Lutheran minister,
six doors down
the polack family
called Polish
on posh days.
Son Joey jailed in
sprung out
ongoing odyssey
straggle-haired mother
pulls Medusan roots
uncoiling Cracowed memories.
Neighbours bite lips
roll eyes
shake heads.

There were respectable ones, there were the DeJonges two doors down ... Mrs. so nice in ample apron stringed to good Mr. DJ not an RC. (But they always get them in the end and Mrs. did.)

"It was a miracle"
Mr. clever chemist
knew all about medicines
kept good health working out
"it was a miracle"
maybe.
The stroke

bedded him for years
she attended
hovering angel
— got him —
in the end.
Then Madeline
only and quiet daughter
finally married
affianced long years
but
got him in the end.
They'd visit
my brothers
time to time
sit over drinks
in the dining room
shyly yet appreciatively
laughing at jokes
I couldn't understand
but knew were dirty
in the dark dining room
where the clothes closet
hid me when I half-tried
hanging myself
maybe I was thirteen
when I wanted to
not really
yet really
made-believe
trying to hang myself
in that deep
deep downstairs
clothes closet
why
I wonder now

it's a miracle
they got me in the end.

My son sent me a recent biography of Thornton, and inscribed it, "In remembrance of some beautiful wet-leaved afternoons in New Haven."

Those afternoons were beautiful. And the leaves did fall, mulching the trees for the long-eveninged winter.

F.L.W.

For the sake of sequence:
I flew to Taliesin West in Arizona after my stint at Yale. This was Frank Lloyd Wright's southern clime — or studio — where Dick had been working with him on plans for the Guggenheim Museum. Come the warmer weather Taliesin West travelled north to become Taliesin East in Wisconsin, a sprawling community-cum-plantation where architecture and rugged farm labour prospered furiously.

Mr. Wright — that's the way he was referred to at Taliesin — and if you were lucky enough to speak with him or be spoken to by him, that's the way he was always addressed: Mr. Wright.

He floats through my memory like a pointillist painting: dot dot dot for his porkpie hat, dot dot dot for that swinging cape, dot dot dot for the accompanying cane. And over the whole image, the soft Wisconsin light ...

It's spring, 1956. The morning's earlier than seven, the green hillside's dew-pearled, and Richard the children and I really believe God's in his heaven and all's right with the world. We scramble from our slapdash quarters recently adapted from the now-vacated pigpens — and so charmingly designed by THE Architect ... or one of his permanent Old Guard ... or paying apprentices ... or visiting architects ... or ... others. I was among the others. Not Dick, however. He'd been received, an architect with licences *in each and every one of the then forty-eight states*.

After my turbulent year at Yale I'd looked forward to an exhilarating change: outdoor life, companionship among artists, and, especially, a wonderland of ART. From high school days I'd saved cut-outs from periodicals, newspapers, essays. And while waiting at rehearsals or between auditions I read everything that marked Frank Lloyd Wright among my ground-breaking twentieth-century innovators. For me at that time, architecture, like theatre, embraced all the arts. It was architecture that had brought my husband and me together in Las Vegas; we used the same technical language describing or critiquing any design: a building, a film, a play, literature. We spoke about levels, texture, space — especially space — and simplicity, honest beauty.

Would I find Ariadne's thread to freedom, to the essence that I called beauty, that organic structure of which Mr. Wright was the standard-bearer? Hmnn hmnn hmnn "Beauty is truth" hmnn hmnn hmnn "truth beauty" hmnn-mnn ... Maybe ... *If* "that is all I ever need to know," what with *my* newly untangled Catholic instruction and my labyrinthine steps, *I'll* marry Christ *and* nature in this creative community! (Row upon row of exclamation points!)

Ah! But there's many a slip between that Cup and my lip. First, what about nature at Taliesin? I'll soon find out. Each day we get our assignments. Not the industrious architects and their co-workers, of course, bent over drawing boards in the studio; their work is focused on the Master's immediate and long-term contracts, revisions by demanding clients that infuriate Mr. Wright, as well as his inspiring sketches for fantastic new projects. We others are required to keep this mill grinding.

The airy outdoors contrasts weirdly with the tension mounting indoors: a huge elastic band ready to snap at *Mrs.* Wright's crisp release. *She* is parsing out our day's labours in carefully acquired English. *Mrs.* W. (Olgivanna) wants us others to find our place — and keep it. *She* was challenged to discover how to dispose of me without disposing of my husband. He was needed. He held all those licences. And was working overtime on the Guggenheim.

A scrim descends over the airy outdoors. We shiver with anticipation. The atmosphere is eerie. I become inflated, deflated, curiously regarded, callously ignored. My mind's eye is like a reversed telescope: as Mr. Wright becomes smaller and smaller, his wife takes on an Andy Warhol brilliance, harsh, flat, gaudy; omniscient and omnipresent. I am a sort of circus curiosity who will take on the roles in which she casts me.

Hausfrau: SEE SARA DUSTING THE GRAND LIVING ROOM RESERVED FOR STATE OCCASIONS. (Once while I was crawling under the back of the grand piano to dust its sturdy legged claws, Mr. Wright came in, sat down in hot fury and played Beethoven — *sforzando* — while I remained motionless, listening until the last crashing chord resounded through my paralyzed body and the Maestro rose imperiously and exited.)

I jump up from my hiding place and race to the windows to claim my freedom, if only by swinging them open to childhood memories of golden fairy fields. That's where I want to be. To hell with the dust of the desert, the dust of the music salon; all the ashes can return to ashes. I kneel on the cushioned bench directly beneath the window, breathe in the sweet fresh air, and listen to the stillness. The scuttlebutt was that if you were good at a job *she*'d keep you at it forever, but if you were bad *she*'d reassign you. Well I was as bad at home care in Taliesin as I was in Vegas. I remember the primitive kitchen where my disasters followed one another, a sympathetic apprentice telling me "Don't say anything, I'll report that you're not fit for kitchen duty, and *she*'ll give you another job until she's satisfied."

Now I once more make a decision: let the dust settle in a few strategic places, forget to empty the vacuum, leave the dead flowers to wither. Maybe I'll be assigned to the vegetable patch! And I was. Hurrah! Another misfit joined me, a charming chap from Karachi. Now the garden patch was more than a patch; in the hot summer sun it was no mean feat for two city-breds to weed carrots all morning. But we were good story-tellers — he of his life in India (before Karachi became part of Pakistan) and his architectural ambitions, I with tales of my acting escapades. By mid-morning of back-breaking weeding we tried a labour slowdown, hiding behind the cabbages. It seemed like a great idea, to avoid sunstroke, get our noses out of the dirt long enough to sit down for a rest and chuckle at our clever tricky plan. But lo

— very low — and behold we were beheld, reported to the *Mrs.*, who reassigned him to washing the barn walls, leaving me to do the onions.

If Taliesin were only a surrealist collage sometimes bordering on nightmare, I would not be painting an honest canvas. There were our children, and following them in Pied Piper fashion their mischievous little companions. Mr. Wright liked children, perhaps Olgivanna did, too, and because the entire adult community was constantly involved with assignments, the children were on their own and they loved it. They were a delight. Free as hummingbirds they flitted wherever the air currents took them. Ours explored undreamed-of nooks and crannies. In the garden patch six-year-old Cathy ate more wild strawberries than her stomach could hold, but that didn't discourage her from trying to eat twice as many little green apples as her basket would hold, cramps notwithstanding. She and eight-year-old Kris sneezed their way through amber waves of corn, all three of us crying help when we weren't able to find each other among the towering stalks.

The alluring beautiful "Romeo and Juliet" windmill FLW had designed at the turn of the century was still standing, unused, a favourite haunt for curious children. One day it almost became a devastating ruin when Kris and Cate and their playmates found a box of dynamite hidden there. Kris raced along the fields to his dad in the drafting room. Holding a dynamite stick aloft he grinned, "Look what I found!" And there, but for the grace of God and Dick's intervention, might have gone the wide-eyed youngsters *and* the internationally famous windmill!

Many of our anxieties were washed away when we all swam under the waterfall in the lake FLW had dammed for water storage. There we laughed our way between snapping turtles, water snakes, and arrogant swans.

My personal contact with Mr. Wright was rare, but one pleasant day we met inadvertently. I was sitting by the fantastic fountain that he'd had imported from Japan when, to my surprise, he joined me. He asked about my dance training with Martha Graham and made a few cutting remarks about her — yet she was as revered in dance as he was in architecture, and as famous. Did he pronounce this anathema on his own or on Olgivanna's behalf? I didn't dare challenge him. He seemed, I thought, respectful toward me and wanted to hear about my theatre experience, and my early dreams of experimenting with form. I wonder now if Olgivanna had delegated FLW to sound me out. Could a niche be found where I might be usefully placed? So that my oh-so-licensed husband could be profitably kept?

Occasionally Mr. Wright appeared in the dining room to share his wisdom, and while he could be repetitive, we didn't mind; he had a wry sense of humour and his oft-repeated anecdotes spanned eight melodramatic comic-tragic decades — and four wives. Once Mr. Wright preached at the "praying hands" Unitarian Church he'd designed in Madison, Wisconsin. I went expecting the heavens to open — and they did, raining down torrents of forgettable ramblings.

Oh God! Christ, don't your nail-hammered hands bleed? Not here at praying hands. Nichevo. And if you prick me don't I bleed? You see, I can't pursue my verb I can't marry Christ with nature where there's no depth, only ego's shallow ritual reserved for sentimental reverencing, a legend still living.

Olgivanna's "spiritual-discipline" had bewildered and revolted me. Silently I found my way out to earliest Mass with the only two Catholic apprentices I knew; they, like the woman who'd helped me in the kitchen, were soon gone from the compound. Surprise! Within a few days after this "secret" escapade *she* asked me, You might like to start a play? — I chose William Saroyan's *The Beautiful People*, cast it, began rehearsals. Great turnout. Most of the people were enthusiastic, especially the apprentices, but after only a few rehearsals word got back to Olgivanna that I was directing, coaching, teaching! Well, no more of that! Taliesin had only ONE teacher and she was THAT TEACHER! I was scaldingly rebuked, assigned to *assist* her approved director for Mr. Wright's eighty-fifth birthday celebration, and told to prepare a "little skit" or two. Her theme was Venice.

Mr. Wright's birthday gifts were to be sailed in from across the man-made lake on a medieval galleon replete with sails and oarsmen. I was to organize the theatrical evening in the small theatre Mr. Wright had designed for films and chamber music. In obedience to *Mrs.* Wright's commands I created an evening of "little" scenes.

For a costumed group I choreographed a few appropriate court dances: a stately pavanne, a racing courante, and, as I remember, a lively bourée. Chamber music and some Shakespeare sonnets provided an *entr'acte* before I performed the prison scene from Maxwell Anderson's Joan of *Lorraine*. It was received in hushed silence — the nicest kind of tribute. After another musical interlude I appeared in medieval dress and brought the audience to a frolicsome climax with Portia's "Quality of Mercy" speech in broad — *very broad* — Brooklynese lingo.

Applause ... cheers ... Mr. Wright rose to his feet, smiling — he really did smile — and, speaking clearly in the hush always granted the Master's words, expressed his delight, said that my evening's contribution inspired his imagination, that he could envision possibilities — or did he say potentialities? — for his Taliesin theatre. He glowed. She didn't. The very next day *SHE* sent Cinderella back to the kitchen.

Again I was a washout; the huge pots were hard for me to handle, but assisting cooking a hundred people's early morning oatmeal gave me invaluable insights into future Gulag incarceration.

I experienced euphoria because of Mr. Wright's tribute. I was excited. I was let down. I still wasn't clear what I was to be or where I was to be in the great world out there. Was I an actor or director, a choreographer, a teacher?

In Olgivanna's view, *nichevo!*

I could not forget that during the time Richard was at Taliesin West in Arizona and I was still at Yale in Connecticut, Olgivanna, he told me, had called him to a private meeting and *demanded* answers to intimate questions regarding our marriage. She encouraged him to choose one of the attractive women in the Fellowship as a temporary stop-gap until I joined him. When Richard, quite startled, said he couldn't square that with God, Olgivanna looked at him without blinking and said, "Here, I am God." So when Richard left Taliesin East for an A.I.A. conference in Venezuela, I, zealous for my new Catholicism, packed up the car and the children and fled in the night to the little town of Spring Green; ran from her powerful, threatening presence.

Why the melodrama, the hysteria, the escape? How did I find the Grubers, the real old Catholic family? Through the priest? Can't remember him, how he looked; the church, its name? *nada* — but the little old nun at her convent door?

Oh yes, there is a real Hell!

Where?

Right there! She said it forcefully, avec *plus de force* — pointing with index finger at the worn squeaking slats on the porch. (I was not invited in; who knows what sinful aroma, sound, image, touch, even taste I might've carried from that place to contaminate if I were offered a glass of water — let alone tea!)

The priest had ordered two women to say the rosary for me. They were audibly scrupulous: Hailmaryfullofgracethelordis — *This is only the second Hail Mary and you're on the third bead; we'll have to start again!* Hailmaryfullofgrace ... *You left a word out. Go back to the beginning* — we were zealots one and all. And Mrs. Gruber? *What would you like for dinner? Would you like chicken and dumplings? Oh yes, please!* Kris and Cathy and I thought that would be one of the nicest treats imaginable. Mrs. Gruber went right out to the backyard, picked up a chicken from her flock and wrung its neck.

How did we get there, where did we sleep, how long did we wait for Richard's return? It took years, perspective, love, to separate the chaff from the wheat. And, like Mr. Wright, Olgivanna has died for history. But not for me; for me she is the essence of fiction.

THE LAST ONE

It is siesta of a May afternoon in the Arizona desert. George Ford Sayers, now an octogenarian, is taking his customary two-hour nap in the bedroom adjoining his wife's. Ludmilla is not napping. She neither lies in her canopied Louis XV bed nor sits in the Sears Roebuck armchair. Ludmilla is on her knees. The ceiling-to-floor magenta drapes are drawn, but a buzzing neon tube-light reveals her motionless.

Her full name is Ludmilla Horny-Sayers. In 1980, while attending a Presidential dinner honouring her husband's contribution to architecture, Ludmilla's ducal ancestry was leaked. By whom is uncertain. It seems that the Russian accented Mrs. Sayers (still referred to behind her back as George Ford Sayers' "last one") was not really Russian at all, but the sole inheritor of the celebrated Horny title of Montenegro.

In a footnote to G.F.S.' *Autobiography of a Genius*, the reader is told that Ludmilla, his fourth wife, was apprenticed to the Royal Ballet of St. Petersburg. But the Bolshevik Revolution interrupted her training. It is not necessary to spend thirty-five dollars on the book to discover this fact. Her tiny feet need no explanation: they are the barely covered bones of an ex-dancer. Her hands, veined and nimble, move swiftly in the air, over surfaces, around objects. When they rest in her lap they have the empty quietness of unused performers. Her high-heeled sandals, worn in varied colours and fabrics every season of the year, expose the bird-like spread of toes, high arch, and narrow ankle peculiar to the naturally formed dancer.

In the silence of this desert estate Ludmilla Horny-Sayers, Duchess of Hornygovynia, is not meditating before an icon in the tradition of her Orthodox Montenegran forebears. No! Her experience as a disciple of the late philosopher Bulieff has raised her above the provincialism of Christianity into the Universality of Reality Society. She'd co-founded it with him in Avignon after the First World War, and continues to lead it from the dry suburbs of Phoenix.

This reverence, then, is not a spiritual exercise. Ludmilla, Duchess of Hornygovynia, is on her knees before the dressing table, not even looking at herself in the mirror. She is listening to the breathing beyond the door that binds her bedroom to her husband's, the one door he has provided as her exclusive exit.

Her head does not turn. Her large brown eyes shift from the mirror to the doorknob. Surgically tightened skin reveals the prominent bone structure of her face. And despite her sixty years, her dyed black hair is groomed precisely as she wore it when she was sixteen in the classic ballet style: parted in the centre, pulled over her ears, and caught at the nape of her neck in a thick chignon. Until recently two strands of white hair were permitted to frame her face. But the new winter's registration in the Horny-Sayers Fellowship has wrought a change of hair colour.

And other things. Vashti, for instance.

Ludmilla presses her thin breast-bone against the dressing table to stop the quivering that her new lover's name generates. The possible Duchess of Hornygovynia has a reputation for a cool head, one that she managed to keep on her shoulders notwithstanding run-ins with the Communists in St. Petersburg, the Nazis during the occupation of France, and the police in the United States when she and G.F.S. were fleeing subpoenas from his third, and at that time undivorced, wife.

Now she is jelly. Her tongue darts over capped teeth that gleam phosphorescently in the darkened room. The taste on her lips evokes memories of Vashti, forcing her eyes from the doorknob to the bed. The three days they had spent in it ended today with G.F.S.' unexpected return from Boston. The man is so undependable!

The metropolis always gives Sayers indigestion, and his attack this time was intensified by a head-on fight with the Board of Directors of his newly designed library. The Board was determined, it seems, to classify the books by the traditional Dewey Decimal System, but the renowned architect was equally determined to have them classified according to colour, size, and shape. There was a stalemate. George Ford Sayers ordered his plane to take off twenty-four hours earlier than planned.

Fortunately his unexpected arrival coincided with Vashti's wish to shower, so when George's massive body swung, cane, cape, and sombrero into Ludmilla's battered bedroom, it was possible for the surprised wife to act every inch the duchess. The running water in the bathroom gave her a chance to excuse herself after the first quick greetings. G.F.S. accepted her explanation that she needed to steam away her insomnia in the old Montenegran fashion, since she'd had a long and very hard three nights owing to her anxiety over his absence.

George withdrew to nap, leaving Ludmilla to extricate Vashti from her bedroom, whose only exit — she repeated over and over to herself on her knees — was through her husband's room.

" " " " "

Vashti sits on the toilet seat, his skin puckered from overlong soaking in the tub. Around his hips is a face-towel, too small for concealment, and plainly marked "Hers." His slender body makes him look younger than his twenty-three years. His undulating muscles are more sharply delineated now than when he came to the Sayers Fellowship six months ago. This is undoubtedly due to the eccentric exercises Ludmilla has taught daily.

Vashti, sitting uncomfortably on the plastic seat, watches water slowly seeping from underneath the tub toward the master's bedroom. Plumbing has never been G.F.S.' strong point. Clients frequently sue him because of misplaced drains and leaking roofs.

At this moment Vashti is very much in sympathy with Sayers' belligerent clients. Soon little puddles will trickle a laboured alarm to the sleeping man and Vashti will find himself out of room, board, favour, and, perhaps, life. He tries to mop the water, but every time he moves the toilet seat creaks and groans. And so Vashti sits still, thinking ...

Vashti was born Sherman Redstone on Grand Street in New York City. He was homeless by the age of four. His father drank his way unsteadily into a cement mixer one night thinking it was the Barrel of Fun at Coney Island. The huge machine was set in motion early the next morning, pouring out Sherman's father permanently distilled and concretely cast.

Sherman's mother didn't brood. With joyful abandon she boarded a tramp steamer as a stowaway and was cared for by the captain until they reached Hong Kong. Not without business acumen, she set up house there, and with the cooperation of the captain and his crew established a cosy place where passing sailors, spies, and salesmen could enjoy their coffee-break.

Sherman, marooned in a tenement hallway, was found by an elderly Indian couple, devoted disciples from afar of Mahatma Gandhi. By day they peddled sweets, by night they conducted an astrology business in their one small room. These idealists saw instantly that the young foundling could, with proper care, be an asset to their way of life.

They renamed him Shah Rajad, fed him fruit, rice, and nuts, sent him to school for a while and put his leisure time to use selling their sweets. The candies appealed to a limited circle. The benefits that accrued to Shah were more fruit, rice, and nuts. Finally, in his eleventh year, they gave him a bed to replace his floor mat.

His new custodians were not without feeling. They taught Shah their native songs, and allowed him to keep the tips he earned when he sang them to the moneyed women and delicate boys who discreetly visited the astrology sessions.

As Shah grew older and taller, the couple began to wonder if the police, or for that matter the boy himself, might suspect that the candies were not all caramel. The couple grew older, too. Their white hairs and bent backs now gave them an innocent appearance. They no longer needed their front man. They let the boy know he was becoming a burden.

At fifteen, Shah had tired of fruits and nuts anyway and took his flute uptown to Greenwich Village. Within a short time his Hindustani love songs were the rage of Washington Square. He was invited to cozy balls and cozier nightclubs.

But soon Shah had to move again. Instead of going farther uptown he left New York entirely, his impetuous imagination aroused by dreams of nature and triggered by the pregnancy of an unemployed dancer. The wide open spaces seemed tempting.

He worked his way westward, casing the tea rooms of Terre Haute, the call-houses of Chicago, and the cheese factories of Wisconsin. He dug mines in Montana and read a book on copper in Colorado. He was getting closer to nature all the time.

In Salt Lake City he heard from fellow shoe clerks that Arizona was a good place to retire. Shah thought about this briefly. No question about it, he was ready to retire. At twenty-three, he was feeling downright old.

It was in Phoenix, then, that Ludmilla discovered Shah polishing glasses at Rico's roadside bar.

Now Ludmilla Horny-Sayers was a vegetarian and a total abstainer. She had learned under Bulieff the value of remaining sober while others drank. This skill became especially important to Ludmilla when she established the Fellowship, a device she shrewdly contrived to offset G.F.S.' outlandish debts, and to provide for the future she was sure to inherit because of the difference in their ages.

G.F.S. gladly allowed his wife to fulfill the role of President, Dean, and Mother Superior, a triune role that she had imagined for herself since Bulieff's mantle had fallen on her shoulders. This left George free for his work, his plans, and himself.

The Horny-Sayers Fellowship *was* Ludmilla's Dominion. Her serfs were a small group of draughtsmen. After their early morning work on G.F.S.' projects she set them to cooking, cleaning, and husbanding the Fellowship's farm and animals. Of course they also studied her mystique of Universality of Reality. No time was wasted. Ludmilla led them in Worship Dance and Edification Hour — a time she set aside for the public acknowledgement of their vices.

On Saturday nights after dinner, the Duchess and her renowned architect husband led invited guests to G.F.S.' private theatre for chamber music and a foreign film. The members of the Fellowship followed, and at evening's end filed past G.F.S.' dais to thank the master for his largesse. With the departure of the celebrities the Duchess of Hornygovynia repealed formalities for the community. The whole crowd took off to Rico's, the bar that was otherwise off-limits. George Ford Sayers retired to bed with his creative dreams. Ludmilla either patrolled the Lion's Gate with her secretary, Miss Peggy, or sometimes made a surprise foray on Rico's.

At the gate, Ludmilla sat next to the lion's head saying her worry beads. Miss Peggy stood between the lion's rear legs reporting in whispered French the arrival of returning students. Miss Peggy conveyed the news with amazing accuracy as she lifted powerful binoculars to powerful bifocals. Situated in this way the two women watched the mating seasons shape themselves. The Horny-Sayers brochure stated clearly that each student would receive unique attention. Ludmilla kept this promise.

On the last Saturday night of October, this mother of the arts, this lover of youth, the Grand Duchess of Hornygovynia, was stationed with Miss Peggy under the lion's legs, a brooding quiet having descended on the three hundred and fifty acres of cacti, rock, and prehistoric mud. The Duchess was restless. She liked romantic films, but tonight's showing starred Anna Magnani in an earthbound Italian story about a starving family who worked in a spaghetti factory. All the characters were killed by the Carabinieri when they tried to steal the uncooked pasta, and the cruel employer salvaged every drop of raw dough from their dying bodies before he kicked them into a donkey's watering trough.

Ludmilla did not like anything that smacked of the proletariat. It not only brought back memories of the Revolution, but memories of her own youth, when, as a usurped Duchess, she had been forced by her parents to contribute to her family's survival by baking bread, weeding the puny onion garden, carrying laundry on her head to a distant stream. It was at this stream that Bulieff had seen her, seduced her, and prophesied a glowing future for her.

Suddenly, as it will in the desert, a roaring wind began to churn, stirring Ludmilla's restlessness to frenzy. She said, "I thirst!" and ordered Miss Peggy to drive her to Rico's.

The place was taken over by the Fellowship, but the noise and excitement subsided for a full sixty seconds when G.F.S.' "last one" made her surprise appearance. Everyone stood. This was customary six days of the week and the reflex was too automatic to rest on the seventh. Ludmilla signalled them to resume their festivities.

She ignored the table that was quickly vacated for her. She walked with sharp clicking steps to the bar and mounted a stool.

"Carrot juice!" said Mrs. Horny-Sayers, and Shah looked into the future. No question about it, he was ready to retire.

Shah had been waiting for this visit. Seven Saturdays had gone by during which he had listened to stories about Ludmilla Horny-Sayers. He'd caught whispered snatches as he served rounds of drinks, picked up odds and ends as he passed from one table to another. At the bar itself had heard the uninterrupted conversation of the older members of the hierarchy, whose prerogative it was to sit at some distance from those who were not of the inner sanctum. He had learned about Ludmilla. He had come prepared.

He slowly put down the beer glass he'd been polishing and studied her face. She was preoccupied and nervous.

He leaned close to her. "Madam," Shah whispered softly, "I have for you this evening something special — borscht flown fresh from Los Angeles."

Ludmilla's huge brown eyes peered directly into Shah's huge brown eyes. They were gripped in magical silence.

"Borscht," she breathed, "and fresh from the west coast. *Mais quelle surprise!* How do you happen to have such a delicacy here?"

Shah bowed low. "Is it not written in Bulieff's *Unpublished Notes* and expanded upon in your own great work, *I Am God*, that each man waits for the thing he loves, but some wait unprepared?"

He raised neither his eyes nor his head, but backed away humbly toward the jar of borscht. His hands reached for a highball glass, and as purple-red juice filled it, he allowed the strains of a Hindustani love song to escape his lips.

"What is your name?" Ludmilla asked as she appraised his curved mouth and slender fingers.

"Shah. Shah Rajad."

"Henceforth you shall no longer be Shah, but Vashti, for all who are of the line are born with me into the Universality of Reality."

And so it was that Vashti qualified for the Fellowship and was received as a candidate for the new semester, which was duly inaugurated on December 25th, Ludmilla's birthday.

The master took to Vashti immediately because he was quiet and eager to please. Ludmilla appointed Vashti G.F.S.' valet and chauffeur. In this way she could supervise his postulancy and he could live in the main house instead of in one of the apprentices' tents.

Vashti blossomed. By January he was promoted to the novitiate. The Ides of March saw the Duchess herself crown him a fully vested member with a wreath of gourds and flowering cacti.

* * * * *

Now he sits in Ludmilla's bathroom paralyzed from having sat so still for almost two hours. Vashti senses that Ludmilla is paralyzed too. No sound comes from her bedroom.

But although Ludmilla is motionless she is not idle. Her scattered thoughts are taking shape. There is always a way out! There was a way out of Hornygovynia, a way out of St. Petersburg, a way out of Avignon. There has to be a way out of that bathroom! True, the small window is too high and narrow even for Vashti's hips; true, too, that the bathroom door, now swollen with steam, will be extremely difficult to open without a terrible racket; and equally true that even if she succeeds in getting Vashti from the bathroom she still has to get him out her one door — the door G.F.S. so cleverly designed to go only through his bedroom. And Vashti not only has to leave, he has to leave dressed.

Ludmilla looks angrily at her floor-to-ceiling windows. To pull the drapes is not an impossibility. They always hitch, hike, and sigh in their passage, but if they are drawn back there is one window panel that could serve — might serve — as an escape hatch. The only difficulty is that although the horizontal slit opens onto the courtyard, she doubts it's sufficiently wide to permit Vashti to slither through. It would be more than mortifying if he were caught half in, half out.

She had told George that Vashti was in Phoenix on an errand. Now the time was approaching when he would awaken and expect Vashti to have returned. George will demand his valet!

She was irritated with George because there was only the one entrance to the room, irritated that he'd arrived a day too early, and irritated beyond all measure that the desert wind had begun its weird howling. Soon it would thrash the pebbles in the courtyard and if they hit the glass windows George would be sure to awaken.

Suddenly there was a violent thunderclap. The noise was deafening. It sounded as if a cannonball had dropped into the centre of Ludmilla's bedroom. In one instant the bedroom door and the bathroom door were flung wide. A sleepy-eyed George and a wide-eyed Vashti were catapulted toward each other in a gush of wind and water.

Mrs. Horny-Sayers shot to her feet. The three stared at each other.

"George!" said Ludmilla.

"Madam!" said Vashti.

George Ford Sayers tried to speak but couldn't. He gesticulated, turned purple, and dropped to the ground.

"Dress quickly," Ludmilla ordered Vashti as she pulled his clothes from a Chinese urn by her bedside.

He did.

"Help me put the old man in his room," she added.

They did.

"Call Miss Peggy and tell her the Master is ill."

When Vashti brought Miss Peggy to the scene, Ludmilla had changed from her negligee to a black mourning gown. Purple sandals adorned her web-like feet. Torrents of rain were falling on the roof and on the pebbles; rain was slashing at the windows, beating on the walls. At the Master's bedside knelt the Duchess of Hornygovynia as if in prayer. Her cheeks were wet, anointed by the water oozing from the Master's leaking ceiling. George Ford Sayers was dead.

The coroner noted that the great architect had suffered a shock as a result of the unusual thunderbolt.

The media described the funeral in exquisite detail: "George Ford Sayers' ashes were tossed over the Fellowship from his private plane while his devoted wife delivered an intense, though composed, oration in Montenegran and a Far Eastern disciple sang a Hindustani requiem."

Once More from the Top
Entr'acte

LONG QUIET BEACHES. The composer percussively scores, creates music for my choreography *Teresa of Avila*, that naughty saint foreshadowing futures drumbeats her life hotly worded in sixteenth-century allusions, scriptural quotes, poet-John-of-the-Cross levitations, and my dancers' elevations. We won't drop said composer's name but let it whimper. That sandy secret cove, together sighing, begging more honey from that honeycomb, the sea's suspiration, our bodies' perspiration plastering my tiny silver holy medal engraved in blue, Immaculate Heart of Mary, ever-virgin against my wet breast, gift from my darling gifted college girls, O! O! O! Immaculate Heart College, what suppurating wounds did you cover at Malibu?

* * * * *

"Mrs. Stadelman," the Registrar began, "I see from your transcripts that you attended The Neighborhood Playhouse."

"Yes, Sister."

"You know we can add that to your credits toward your degree."

"Thank you — "

"It also says you studied dance."

"Yes. With Martha Graham, Sister, and — "

"Some of our girls here have been clamouring for some … is it … modern dance?"

"Yes, Sister."

"Do you know it?"

"Oh yes."

"Would you be willing to do a little something for us?"

"Of course, Sister."

"A few extracurricular classes? It would have to be voluntary of course."

"Of course."

I was Catholic now.

* * * * *

Ah Lydia, ah Virginia! And that lovely Philippina girl. Why does time erase all those other names? Six or eight, maybe ten of us met in an empty room after classes. I hadn't danced in twelve years. I had to limber up while I taught. Those girls were so talented, so enthusiastic. Word seeped out. Or maybe nuns had ways of peeking in. Immaculate Heart, after all, was their college.

* * * * *

I was a part-time student, something I was everywhere we went, Richard, the children, and me. I took Sister Humiliata's course, *The Divine Comedy*. She was a great teacher, had a sabre-sharp mind and a profile that was a dead ringer for Dante. One day she stopped me after class. She, too, must have heard about the "dancers."

"Mrs. Stadelman, the big feast of our Order is coming up on December eighth. Would you consider creating something with your dance group that we could present in the auditorium, something to celebrate the Immaculate Conception?"

"Well yes, Sister ... "

I had only one reservation. I hadn't a clue what the Immaculate Conception was.

* * * * *

These nuns I'd been meeting in Los Angeles were exceptional women, exciting company. So I kept my ignorance to myself. I'd only taken instruction in the Catholic faith a few months before at Yale. What was the Immaculate Conception? Was it something real? Or even possible?

Scripture would be the source! There I had an advantage. Few Catholics of the fifties were as familiar with the Bible as the average Christian Scientist who read it daily!

But the Bible shed no light upon such a confusing, confounding dogma. Rome's sophistic, mind-boggling interpretation of Mary's "Immaculate Conception" is still confused by many Catholics with her immaculate conception of Jesus. The story of Mary's *fiat*, however, was familiar to me and I wanted to celebrate it.

Something was happening. The glamour of performing on Broadway, in Vegas, and on the war front had long been tarnished. But here was a spark back again. Mary's life, theology aside, was epic stuff. It was, by God, "the joy of my youth!"

I couldn't deal with the troublesome dogma, but I could rely upon my artistic instincts and my erstwhile Protestant independence and individual interpretation of the Bible. I created a twenty-five-minute dance-drama called *The Magnificat*. The Scriptural text describes the visit of the newly-pregnant Virgin to her cousin, Elizabeth (The Visitation). I expanded that to include the earlier Scriptural scene in which the Angel Gabriel appears to Mary (The Annunciation). With artistic licence and spiritual boldness I choreographed the Angel as an emanation of the Holy Spirit.

There was no scenery. To propitiate any ultra-conservative nuns, we used wrap-around skirts over tights and leotards, and capped our heads with small kerchiefs.

My Virgin was a beautiful diminutive Phillipina. She lay on the floor, her body open, arched in a Graham release. My Gabriel/Holy Spirit was an exquisite six-foot dancer. In the Annunciation scene she reached one leg over the Virgin Mary, her pointed foot describing a circle that developed into an arabesque, and came to rest in a second position plié astride the Virgin. It was good. Spectacular. It was 1956!

* * * * *

December 8th. College Auditorium:
A seat in the row behind me pops up. There is a serpentine hissing. I turn and see an old nun scrambling toward the aisle spitting "Sacrilege! Sacrilege!" It unnerves me. I look

back at the stage. How could this beauty be sacrilege? Then I receive another shock when the performance ends: a resounding ovation literally shakes the auditorium.

Backstage Sister Humiliata surprised me. She introduced me to Father Patrick Peyton, the internationally famous rosary evangelist. To Catholic girls he was that day's megastar. He was also a saint, despite his maladroit slogan, "The family that prays together stays together." He was tall, smiling, a silver-haired Irishman whose robust appearance — contradicting his chronic tuberculosis — impressed me so much that I wasn't prepared for the soft sad keening voice:

"Och this was a mighty praise, Och this is something to please our Holy Mother. Would you let me give you a blessing now."

I was stunned when he gave me a special blessing for what he called "your work."

* * * * *

A spiral staircase uncoiled. It wasn't as I'd supposed, up, up, down, down. Its twists and turns straightened the line from Brooklyn to Broadway, from war zones to Vegas, and all the intersecting levels; naughtiness and niceness, marriage and children, red, green, and yellow lights, bridges over troubled, placid, and often muddied waters. In going forward I was facing backward. Events had swirled past leaving little time to watch my footsteps. I'd forgotten that I'd choreographed before!

Now the sisters wanted *The Magnificat* repeated for an invited audience of parents, benefactors, and friends. The twenty-five-minute presentation would have to be expanded, so I was asked to speak. The performance proved to be an event. This was Hollywood, and there were several celebrities, among them the noted Bauhaus architect, Richard Neutra. The applause was deafening. My performers were nonplussed. So was I at what we'd achieved. We'd added a question-and-answer period. Richard Neutra had one: "Are you too tired to repeat this inspiring piece?" We repeated it.

A Los Angeles TV station offered Immaculate Heart College something unheard-of in the fifties, when equipment was heavy, almost immovable — an hour-long remote program to be telecast from the campus. The producers' only proviso was that they focus on my classes. I didn't have any. The dance class was extracurricular. I wasn't on the faculty and my work wasn't listed in the curriculum. Still, Immaculate Heart College was beginning a massive expansion fund drive, and there could be no better opener than a free hour on TV. My new work was to have screen time in Hollywood!

I was called to the president's office. "Oh dear what can the matter be?" I hummed. Questions ran through my mind as I skimmed polished corridors that smelled of lemon wax and gleamed like ice: Could my volunteer dancers be failing their grades? Did Sister Thecla know about the old nun who'd stomped out of the theatre and was heard later whispering to one of her few friends, "I know where that woman got the disgusting position she used in *The Magnificat* with that girl squatting over the Virgin. From that filthy movie, *The Birth of a Baby*."

"That woman" had never seen *that* filthy movie, but long after 1956 did see the Christ-figure sculpted above Chartres Cathedral's main portal. In *that* same second-position plié. And with His right hand raised in blessing!

Sister Thecla. Her Ph.D. from Oxford intimidated me. I didn't yet have a B.A. from anywhere. She was slender, small and lovely, always dignified on campus, completely at home in her native Hollywood Hills. But in the privacy of her office she had a chronic need to ease the pinching of the starched coif on her red-splotched skin. In a few years she would be dead of skin cancer.

"I've decided that it would be prudent to observe protocol and inform Cardinal MacIntyre of our television plans. Will you go with Sister Humiliata to see him, Mrs. Stadelman?"

* * * * *

We were on time for our appointment. We were announced. Sister Humiliata preceded me. We genuflected to kiss Cardinal McIntyre's ring. An idolatrous act in my former Calvinist circles was now converted to high drama: the Cardinal's presence in scarlet regalia, rippling satins, gold pectoral cross encrusted with coloured stones. Overwhelming.

Sister did the talking. The Cardinal leaned forward, listening.

"To hear and see the Blessed Mother onstage, Your Eminence, gave us new insights ... " She hesitated.

"These were the girls' parents, Sister?"

"They were parents, Your Eminence, patrons and friends, *many* of them non-Catholic."

He smiled.

"The dance-drama emphasized the importance of the Virgin Mary's role in *today's* world."

"Yes," said the Cardinal, mindful of his own banking family's prominence in that world. "I can see how that would enlarge the College's contacts and reputation. You are in the midst of your fund drive, aren't you?"

Sister took a deep breath. "Your Eminence, that's what's so promising. Not only have the dancers performed a beautiful work based upon Scripture and ancient litanies, but word has gone out that Immaculate Heart College now offers a broad and attractive curriculum."

The Cardinal smiled.

Sister beamed.

My heart thumped. God, this was theatre!

The Cardinal's cape rustled as he rose. We knelt to receive his blessing. But from the far side of his enormous desk he did a slow, troubled double-take.

"Sister, did I understand you to say that Our Blessed Mother ... DANCES?"

Sister Humiliata persisted with diplomatically downcast eyes, "This little play is performed with great dignity and reverence."

A moment of monastic silence.

"Oh *Sister*, I'm afraid the people aren't ready for that yet!"

We left without a word. Sister Humiliata led me by the hand to the parking lot. In the next Dante class she caught my eye as she quoted the poet's line, "The miracle of the church is that it survives despite its ministers."

And Sister Humiliata had other ideas up her habit's long sleeve.

"Why not take a whirl with Teresa of Avila, Mrs. Stadelman?" She referred me to Marcel Auclair's popular biography of the Spanish saint.

I read, I researched, I fell in love with that Counter-Reformation fighter. Avila's Teresa de Ahumeda meant business and raked a few corrupt religious orders over the coals. She burned her imprint on the Church that tried to forget her, tried to stop her, but couldn't.

Banners flying, we began production. No costume department existed, but without fanfare the nuns and volunteer helpers cut, sewed, fitted my bevy of newly termed "dancers" in blazing red, orange, bright yellow. Teresa herself wore that vibrant liturgical green for hope, her ample swirling skirt lined with scarlet, reminding us that Teresa, too, had "come a long way, Baby." (*Time* was to use that slogan a few years later on its cover story about these same nuns.) To the accompaniment of castanets and freshly-minted baroque music arranged for xylophone, drums, and bells by the sand-pounding composer, my "girls," like Saint Teresa, emerged as the women they were, and Teresa de Ahumeda emerged with them a fully-dimensioned woman, her psyche and sexuality intact.

* * * * *

Blue sunshine, steady waves rolling, rolling, dragging seaweed and shells and the smell. Above our swank shanty traffic sizzles with hot tar; salt spray blends familiar fumes, dead fish, barbecued entrails, empty beer-foamed mugs. We drive to and fro into Hollywood, Immaculate Heart College. Nuns of all ages, medievally-aged in habits dim black and lustrous blue, look sweetly starched but white around the gills, coifs circle pinched faces. Only Sister Jane, Giacometti-thin, floats through the corridor carrying one thorn-pricked rose as long as her flowing robe.

* * * * *

Ave Maris Stella ... Star of the sea, mixed up with our place at Malibu, the pretty little chapel perched on top of one of the hills, our enthusiastic attendance at Mass, newly converted zealots singing at the tops of our voices on a Sunday morning, the sleek friendly seals slithering on the rocks near our little sandcastle, sunning themselves.

Malibu and those tiny grunions appearing once a year, driving everyone mad in moonlight trying to net them, never succeeding. Those hot salty afternoons when, in my hausfrau impersonation, I stood basting a pot roast, dreamily casting my eyes to the rolling waves, those inviting waves away from the kitchen heat, and saw — SAW — my husband lying with a huge Anita Ekberg-like blonde goddess — well, not lying with her, but sun-bathing with her in very close, "intimate," shall we say, conversation, and I threw the entire pot, pot roast pungent sauce and all, right at them. (Coming from Brooklyn I pitched and struck the bitch. Well ... I pitched the pot and hit a home run. At least she ran home and he ran in, first into the Pacific to rinse off the tomato-garlic sauce, and then into our hot house, which grew hotter by the minute.)

Ave Maris Stella ... Star of the Sea ...

* * * * *

The dismal memories of the Bird Cage Theatre's failure receded. I was no longer Mrs. Noah, but had, god-like, regained importance and authority. I was sailing along in a special ark, grateful to Mr. Noah for his admiration and loyalty, which kept us afloat. Of course, on board there was that playful goat whose antics scored with his original music for *Teresa of Avila*.

This second production was a breakthrough in Catholic Theatre. I still used the traditional off-stage narrator, but onstage the performers spoke and chanted key words and phrases. I was winding my way, the form not yet found as I grappled with heroic content in my imagination. We were sent to the National Catholic Theater Conference in Kansas City. Hundreds of nuns, priests, and students representing colleges and schools throughout the country heard Teresa's words animated by modern movement. Bare legs leaped, syncopated falls and recoveries opened eyes of audiences previously blind to the body's beauty when Teresa cried, "Why should we say devil! devil! when we can say God! God!"

Direct and Alternating Currents

I AM A LITTLE GIRL, PERHAPS SIX OR SEVEN. I stand by my tall bedroom window facing the flat tin roof that spreads over the kitchen below. It is sunset. Am I really so miserable because I've been chastised, or because I like to be miserable, dramatic? They say I'm another Sarah Bernhardt. *They* are my mother and her family and friends whom I amuse, and sometimes — maybe frequently — insult with sharp impersonations.

Why do I escape to the bedroom that I bitterly share with my sister who is ten years older than me? I hate. I yearn. Fairy stories ignite my imagination. I look at the setting sun, a round orange glowing winter ball, and I want to be that boy in the story I have just finished reading. I follow him to a golden house with golden windows leading us on and on to a home of fantastic promise. But oh! we keep walking over nettled hills to this home, an ever-receding place that doesn't exist. Each house that we come to is leaden, dull. We must keep walking to the next. Surely the promised house with the shining glass windows is waiting for me, the home where everything is open to receive me. But the walk is endless.

That boy in the story must face the awful truth: the golden peaceful place is a mirage, fading with the setting sun. That child must learn there's "no place like home." Must he also learn to be satisfied with its emptiness?

I won't. No. I try to catch the sun's last hot beams. I push the flaming circle back where it belongs. Stay there! I have something important to tell you. I'm going to be a great actress. Or a great dancer. I pledge, I promise, I make a promise forever-or-hope-to-die. I will be, I will be, I will be OUT, AWAY, far AWAY where it is golden beautiful, waiting for me. No epileptic crippled sister, no abusive quarrelling family, no loud wrangling shouting voices. (Somewhere over the cliffs ... the rainbow.)

* * * * *

Sure, Teresa of Avila said why should we say devil, devil, when we can say God, God; that was her direct current. But she also said, "I felt as if I were being torn apart. Against my will." That was her alternating current. And sure, too, I had begun to identify with the passions and struggles of women who were almost bigger than life and Teresa de Ahumada was BIG. I felt I knew her. Sure!

I sensed that I was on a new creative adventure. The house with the golden windows was here with the Catholics and their big women saints. The Catholics' *au courant* dictum was Father Patrick Peyton's: "The family that prays together stays together." We bravely challenged that. We could be together and separate. I was sure of that, too. Richard was going to be supervising architect for the new American Embassy in Athens, Greece. Son Kris would go with him. My little daughter and I would nestle together five thousand miles from them at Catholic University in Washington, D.C. My acquiescent, adoring husband submitted to my dream, perhaps my vision. I thought it was that, although I had only a sketchy idea of what I was envisioning.

Teresa of Avila had been a hit in Kansas City. Father Hartke, President of the National Catholic Theater Conference, was also Chairman of the Drama Department at Catholic University. He was rapturous:

"When will you be coming our way?"

"Which way, Father Hartke?"

"East, of course! My drama students need some fresh insights into experimental theatre." He smiled beguilingly. "We don't have any staff openings at present, but let's keep in touch and if you ever come to Washington, maybe we can work something out."

Ah! A golden window.

That's where Father Thomas Dominic Rover surprised me. He'd been posted to the Dominican House of Studies in Washington. He recognized my loneliness, my longing to create something special. He became my Spiritual Director, filling the void left by the missing half of my family. He stepped into my life again, not with a giant stride, but with carefully measured walk and a pedestrian gift: a book about a late-nineteenth-century saint, Thérèse of Lisieux. I had been enraptured with the dynamic Spanish Teresa of Avila; this was the autobiography of a passive French nun with the sentimental sobriquet of "The Little Flower." True, both were Carmelites, but there the comparison ended. He'd inscribed the book, "Stay close to Thérèse and her Master, and be little, and die with them, and find peace forever!"

"Die with them?" Good heavens! What was he wishing me, this smiling Dominican on whom I counted for witty exchanges, literary references and ever-so-subtle spiritual guidance? He was a friend, my only close friend in Washington, and he knew I respected him enough to labour through any book he recommended. But!

He watches as I set the table, put the teakettle on, fold Cathy's socks and winter leggings.

"I pick her up at St. Anthony's. She likes to come with me to see my girls' movement classes. When we get back from the studio she and her nine-year-old boyfriend Francis spend the rest of the afternoon outside in the snow 'playing Mass.'"

"You ever take time to breathe?" Father said.

"Not really. While supper's cooking, I try to get back to the script I've been writing about Francesca da Rimini. Thought it might appeal to the drama students. But it isn't working."

"Yeah," he laughs. "That's why I thought maybe you need some time out. To think."

He leaves after the ritual tea and biscuits and obediently I begin reading Thérèse de Lisieux' autobiography, *The Story of a Soul*.

"Dull, dull, Dull!" I tell him on his next weekly visit. "I'm grateful for your gift, Father Thomas Dominic, but this gal and I are not meant for each other. She never *does* anything! Just prays and contemplates and prays and suffers and contemplates and suffers. Oy!"

"Yes, yes," Father laughs, "Like *The Divine Comedy*, it's all about love."

"Nineteenth-century religiosity," I interrupt.

"As an act of obedience to your Spiritual Director," Father Rover whispers, "try reading it through again."

Cathy comes rushing in, too excited to speak, holding two frost-covered pine cones in mittened hands. We hug her and make a silent ceremony of placing her icicled gifts next to the frozen window.

Over three weeks and as many visits I tried following the little French Carmelite's spiritual journey and, parable-like, after three times, was about to give it up when I caught a flickering light as tiny as the saint herself. "I want to be a saint," she'd said. "Not a great one, just a little one. I've found my vocation. It's love."

I told Father T.D., "I understand why you are so moved by St. Thérèse; she is lovely."

Father opened his hands as if he were about to invoke a blessing. "I think you can do something with her story."

"No. Look. Teresa of Avila sprung from the Baroque Spanish Counter-Reformation, bold, daring, fierce. She pushed and fought and managed to found convents. Her friend, St. John of the Cross, *fled* the Inquisition. Teresa the radical reformer weathered it. But little Thérèse of Lisieux is stationary, stays in one place, lies dying at the age of twenty-four. No movement. No drama. Well, surely, no *dance-drama*."

"Maybe you can find a way."

Way was the operative word. I don't know if my friend deliberately used that word, or even if I had been aware of its precise application to my work, but "the way" became the road I would travel, the streets I would walk to and from the apartment where I read, studied scripture, and prayed. We had no car and it seemed it was always winter in the cold studio where I worked alone to prepare classes for my diligent students.

* * * * *

I stretch and bend at the barre, leave it, sit on the floor, crouching, folding and unfolding my back, my legs; get up, jump in place, run around the room slowly, words keeping time with my sliding, rising, leaping, falling. Not the usual counting sounds, breathing gasps, victorious shouts or frustrated grunts. I turn one way and then another, with words — silly, mawkish ones — "I want to be a saint." Ha! She wants or I want what? To be a saint? "To be a saint." Hop, hop from one foot to the other.

She says/I say, "God doesn't call those who are worthy." I jump, fall, contract fiercely, cry, "Not those who are worthy," I release, arch back, way back, "but those God chooses!" I open my hands, loosen my fingers. Back to my life, not hers, not that little bitsy "Thérèse, the Little Flower," but me, wretched wrenched weed.

My revulsion is no longer against Thérèse, but against the Victorian sentimentality imposed upon her stature. She's no "*little* flower." She's as big as Avila, fierce and focused on a single-minded goal. "My vocation is *love*!" And she lives it while nuns surround her with scorn and contempt; she is a fire burning itself to a last blaze.

There's repeated knocking at the studio door. I scramble to my feet. Hellos, halloos, welcomes. My beautiful drama students come in from the storm, pile their boots, coats in a corner, stand before me eagerly awaiting a workout and maybe, today, rehearsals for that mysterious play she hints at.

Yes, dear young bewildered friends who one by one have secretly told me about your love affairs (this is still the fifties, we're Catholic, you know, and it's tough being a virgin): Pauline is passionately in love with her step-brother, is that incest? Brenda is a lesbian, should she confess it and try to change? Liz, O! Liz vigorously pulls at her leotard crotch, catches my eye and laughs out loud: How much longer can I keep my black lover's visits secret from my mother?

"Today, girls, gals, ladies, women, we're going to penetrate the word *love*."

Silence, disciplined behaviour before authority. What does she have in mind, must be Shakespeare. Nervous giggle from one embarrassed throat.

"I'm going to speak a line here, a word, a phrase from the autobiography of a saint."

Relief wafts over the now heated studio. I can almost hear, Safe, we're safe! Whew! Back in the familiar theological cocoon.

"Let's start with Thérèse of Lisieux' own struggle. She's about your age when she says, 'God refuses me the shadow.'"

The group gathers behind me, bare feet follow mine, quietly. Again Thérèse: "Love is all the skill I have ... when I speak of penance, I don't mean the kind practised by great saints.

Sensational acts of piety are not for me. Love is my vocation but I'm only at the foot of the ladder." They repeat the words after me as they repeat the movements I explore with them. My hands grasp a partner and we run under a shelter of upraised, linked arms. I begin to choreograph consciously, clearly.

"Liz, your line: 'One must have travelled the same sunlit tunnel to realize how dark it is.'" I begin to cast and to direct the play. Biblical scripture, litanies, prayers, weave in and around Thérèse's dialogue. My dancers have become speaking actors, electric conduits for a twentieth-century flashing light: "The way is love! Find the way! God doesn't call those who are worthy but those whom He chooses."

* * * * *

My play, *The New Canticle*, captures Catholic University's theatre audience. Is it dancers acting or actors dancing? Whatever it is, it happens all at once.

My actors danced and dialogued simultaneously without break or interruption in character or storytelling — no pantomime or representational portraiture. My direction had penetrated Thérèse's interior life so specifically that it could be performed and understood. This was drama, epic drama.

Critics called it a new kind of theatre. At first I referred to it as "soul-sized."

I believed I'd found my spiritual and artistic home. Every window was golden.

Ariadne Sleeps/ Artemis Splits

1958:
Maria, on her hands and knees, vigorously polishes the wood floors. She doesn't see me, or if she knows I'm there doesn't want to be interrupted. I stand at the archway to the living room long enough for her to sense my presence.

"Madam?"

"Mmmm," I smile, shaking my head, "*Ochi*," remembering one of my three-word Greek vocabulary — no; I want nothing and turn away.

This is my first bittersweet day in Greece.

Our rented home, actually an imposing villa careless of space, stands square, stuccoed, pocked with hunks of coloured stone. It dominates the beach-front. In every room sun-shafts dart across bowls of purple and yellow blossoms, all gathered by Maria and my two young children.

The noon heat is to be fended off behind wooden slats. I can hear Maria closing them.

There is a museum atmosphere: hushed space, over-stuffed furniture, the smell of lemon-scented wax Maria applies to the parquet floors.

The hallways have marble floors. I follow them to the open French doors, look out to the Aegean Sea and the long rock dock that stretches back to our verandah. I feel a crazy elation, the hysterical freedom I tried to temper last evening by burying my head in my children's sweet-smelling hair. I'd reached out to my husband, who touched me hungrily but seemed to recede from view as I looked beyond his body to the shimmering island of Aegina.

Now the midday light blinds me and the heat drugs me.

What is there for me to do?

Go upstairs, be alone, start to write as I'd planned. Up. Up. Up. *Ephano*, up. Remember down is *cato*. Up, down. *Ephano, cato*. Labyrinthine stairs leading to so many split-levels. Ariadne ... I'm not in a hurry. Time ticks away persistently. I wonder what Maria will be doing downstairs when I reach the landing, when I reach the room, when I sit at the desk and face the gaping typewriter. And the window.

I push the worn flat desk tightly against the window. I'd hoped that window would be my view-finder. I see one sailboat tacked on as an afterthought to the tantalizing Aegean Sea.

Yesterday Maria insisted I keep the window closed because of the heat. Was that what she meant when she fanned the air and said, *Zesto*?

* * * * *

But yesterday was a festival of celebration, a tumultuous family reunion. My twelve-year-old daughter Cathy and I docked in Piraeus to join my husband and son after a six-month separation. We were still feeling the shock waves of our noisy half-hour drive to this place in Glyfada. Dick and Kris excitedly pointed out the clutter of fishing smacks, launches, and yachts, the taverna that cooked the best octopus and served the best ouzo. And Cathy and I were to meet Maria, praised in every letter, "the find of a lifetime, housekeeper, caretaker, cook," and above all, surrogate mother to my fourteen-year-old Kris: "She supervises his piano practice!"

It's curtain time. My mouth's dry. What are my lines?

The door opens. Maria — or is it Medea? — crisply aproned white-over-black uniform, curtsies to her untried mistress, kisses my hand, murmurs what my pounding ears guess is welcome, and presents me with a fresh garden bouquet.

"Madam," she whispers, and takes charge, ushering us into the bright salon, where trays laid with china and silver hold a steaming pot of "cafe," she says, and "leemonahde," for "Kristoki-mo" and "Katerina."

"O excellent," I say, "Greek — *Elenika* — coffee." I emphasize *Elenika* to pay homage.

"*Ochi*, *ochi*, no, no *Elenika* cafe," she smilingly corrects me; "*Turrrrrkeshi cafe!*"

Four hundred years of hated occupation happily overlooked because of the coffee. I have been shown my place.

* * * * *

I begin fingering the typewriter keys, tap tap tap. And there is a tap tap tapping on the window, a hummingbird in the oleander tree below the sill. *Exo!* Don't you know a writer is at work? I type the date, upper left-hand corner, add my name. If I can contrive a paragraph, Maria will hear the sounds, believe I'm working.

There's a hesitant knock at the door. Maria. Do I need anything? Cafe. *Tchai? Ochi, parokala*, no thank you. I point out the window, say *oreo*, beautiful. I mean the hummingbird and the oleander. Maria says, *Zoe*. I think she's correcting me. I repeat, *Zoe?* The bird? The tree? We struggle with our frustrating pantomime, laugh, chant *Zoe*, *zoe*, and fall giggling into each other's arms. She goes back to her work.

I'm bored out of my skull. I sweep my few papers to one side, slam the cover down on my typewriter, push the chair against the desk and run downstairs. Burning hot, I put on a bathing suit and plunge into that seductive sea, take long strokes, but the sun, that unyielding Attic light, pursues me. I turn back for a few seconds, look at the empty beach, dive under again, churn the salt sea-water with my beating feet. I can't stop thinking, am too tired. Spit salt.

Heavily I drag my body back to land, past Maria's searching eyes (she seems to have a way of peering from behind half-closed doors), lurch to my bedroom, draw the drapes against that goddamned sun.

Night: the children asleep, Maria guarding them like the stalwart Palace guard, *evzone*, my husband and I leisurely walk the wooden boardwalk — the *paralais!* — to his favourite taverna on the waterfront. We take off our shoes, dip our feet in the sea, munch a cheese *taropita*, drink cold beer and praise the gods. Dick increases my vocabulary: *Zoe* means life.

* * * * *

Early morning, perhaps five o'clock, and shouting such as we are not accustomed to hearing in this posh suburb. Clearly these male voices are not drunk; they're shouting directions. Fierce, explosive commands. Barefoot, I go to the window, carefully draw back an inch of curtain to see with my barely opened eyes fishermen rushing back and forth hauling nets, lifting baskets bulging with their fresh catch. The excitement is tremendous; this is no ordinary event.

What are they doing setting up market on *our* dock? My eyes widen to follow their gesticulating, their garbled yelling, now impatient, now cajoling, up — *ephano*, *ephano* — up a ramp ... to ... my eyes are opened now ... to an unimaginably gigantic yacht!

I dress quickly, shorts and shirt, run outdoors, not daring to get in the way of the heaving, hauling workers who I now see are delivering not only fish, but crates of fruits, vegetables, and boxes, boxes, boxes of fresh breads and pastries. Sweet and pungent smells intermingle with the fresh salt air.

Restraint isn't possible a minute longer. I'm a foreigner in Greece, but I'm also the proprietor of this villa, that dock. I push through the workmen, make myself visible with gestures and a few frenzied Greek words demand, *What* is that? — pointing to the invader, that awesome white whale — *Who* is at our dock without permission? I stamp my foot. Picking up one inert fish that has dropped from his basket, a sweating fisherman near me hisses over his shoulder, "Onassis! And Garraboo," he angrily adds, "Greeta Garraboo."

We hear later that Churchill is also on board, but by that time the boat has finished with us and moved on.

So the beach in front of our villa in Glyfada is not altogether private. There's Niki, a handsome twelve-year-old on the impish side, who, when he finds no one to keep him company, strips off his trousers and dives in, his underpants quickly submerging as he beats the water with strong brown arms, occasionally tossing a swirled conch to shore. I often see him ambling the *paralais*, probably skipping school. Casual, cocksure, he leans against a post, Lolita-like, smiling at older men who shoot their cuffs and reach for their pockets. I discourage my youngsters from playing with him after school when jellyfish and stingrays lure them to explore the waterfront. Niki knows where to find and how to tease the sea-creatures.

During siesta time when all traffic is hushed and no one walks the *paralais*, Maria makes her way to the deserted beach. Fully dressed and carrying a large towel, she stops, looks to the right and left, and proceeds to shake out her towel. She throws it across her shoulders and under its shroud, strips. She steps out from the modest puddle of her clothes and rushes into the sea, heavy legs flailing, black knotted chignon unexpectedly unwinding and streaming behind her as she breast-strokes quickly away from shore.

She doesn't know I am watching from my upstairs window, doesn't know I'm wondering what she's thinking as she swims. Is it of her soldier fiancé, Captain Georgos, or of planning tonight's dinner for the four of us, or is she thinking of her family on the island of Tinos, where just a few generations ago her ancestors were exiled by the Turks because they had the misfortune to be Roman Catholics?

I turn away to my desk, go back to the waiting typewriter and that window kept immaculately polished by Maria. I'm transfixed by my reflection in it. My lips mirror silent questions: What's my verb? Am I to play the Vegas role again? Addenda to my handsome architect husband? Drinking partner at the scheduled cocktail parties? I've noted them on the Cyrillic calendar in the villa's kitchen pantry, which Maria has unsmilingly indicated is her territory.

The children at school, Dick at his job, Maria quietly at work in the lugubrious, sprawling villa.

What am I to do?

Teach theatre to the Greeks?

Po-po-po, as the Greeks say with a raised-eyebrow shrug. Couldn't I inveigle a director to let me choreograph? Are they, in 1958, into contemporary dance?

Off I drive through Athens' mad traffic and bewildering squares, around pedestrians who turn their backs to oncoming cars, taking chances rather than forfeiting freedom.

Suddenly, up from jumbled heaps of sand-coloured buildings, the Acropolis rises. Silent woman.

Standing.

Fast-forward: we visit Sunion and the temple of Poseidon. Now rewind: we go to Olympia, our guide's anger fanned by the constant stream of archaeologists. "Barbaric Germans!" he says. "We defeated them ten years ago. Of course they're doing so much restoration, *and* paying for it!"

I feel myself included in his cold condemnation of the Christian barbarians who he claimed had destroyed the original Olympia, neglecting to mention that it has also been subjected to natural devastation, earthquakes, fires.

We sailed to Patmos. Noble rock. A few hundred white houses crouched in its clefts. On its peak the monastery circled St. John's cave. The landscape and the seascape both clearly demanding that the Apocalypse be written on that island. For me it was as if he still walked in the light surrounding the island, not brooding or hovering, but resting, waiting to resume revelation.

I experience a strange time-warp, a new kind of travel, a voyage in faith.

I am driving along a rarely used road. I stop to rest in a little fishing village. There are a few scattered dwellings and a small round church, washed dazzling white. The rough wood doors are open, so I step inside. Bare curved walls focus my attention on an intricately painted altar screen — an "iconostasis" — separating the sanctuary from the congregation. This one is special. Its vibrant colours draw me. I'm not prepared to find such artistry in a remote village.

There are no pews. I sit on the earthen floor, glad to be alone; especially glad there's no one to shoo me away, or trap me in strange worship services. I just want to look at the altar screen, at the fiery Christ figure and the parable of the faithful servant.

The silence is so soothing that my eyelids begin to close, my head sags. Almost in time with my breathing, like last thoughts before sleep, questions inch themselves in and out of my mind: All this beauty ... who created it where does it come from ... how did it find its way here ... how did *I* find my way here?

Suddenly, out of the silence comes a deep rumbling sound like the bottom string on a bass viol. It grows louder and richer. It's a human voice chanting words I can't understand but sense are prayers.

I have the uncanny feeling the voice is coming from that living Christ on the iconostasis. It lifts me to my feet.

At that same moment a tiny figure comes from behind the screen, an aged, black-clothed priest. He continues chanting until he sees me. Then we're both stock-still. I can't believe where that huge voice has come from, and he can't imagine where I've come from!

But he is smiling. He looks at me questioningly. I point to the Christ and whisper the only Greek word I remember. "*Oreo*" — Beautiful! He comes down from the altar, his arms wide in welcome, and in broken French asks if I am a Catholic. In school-girl French I murmur, "*Oui, mon père, mais ...,* " and make the sign of the cross in the Roman Catholic manner to indicate our differences. "*Attendez,*" he says, and vanishes behind the screen. I wait.

There is a rustling, then the priest reappears in full vestments singing "*Kyrie Eleison, Christe Eleison*" — that one Greek phrase still kept in the Roman Catholic rite! Piece by piece, in pantomime, he explains the meaning of each vestment, then disappears once more behind the iconostasis.

This time he comes out carrying a large circular bread stamped with crosses and the Greek letters *Alpha* and *Omega* — the Beginning and the End. He blesses the bread and with a small dagger cuts it. He holds it toward me. "*Fayeto!*" (Eat!) he says.

I kneel and receive the Eucharist that we both believe to be the Body of Christ. "*Amen*," he thunders, "*Amen!*"

Quietly I leave the church. "*Madame*," the priest calls after me. He points to an elderly woman in a nearby doorway. "*Ma femme*," he says. His wife slowly approaches me. In one hand she holds a spoonful of fruit preserve, in the other a cup of water. "*Fayeto!*" she commands; "*Kala!*"

* * * * *

Greece was a frantic panorama. Just one damn thing after another.

Trauma.

Meeting writers in some office, not really knowing what we wanted of each other, suspecting each other's motives. The fear, always the fear of the Red Scare following us from Vegas.

Dick's contract as supervising architect for the U.S. Embassy in Athens was terminated, or rather, not renewed. Whatever was the real cause — his return to alcoholism after we'd left the Christian Science Church or my naive political sympathies — we never knew. One year of beauty and turmoil. I needed a Theseus thread to untangle my terror and lead me to creativity.

Back to the desk! The old typewriter waits like a gaping mouth. I'm to spoon-feed it? — a play, a poem, a story, an essay?

I find a psychiatrist. On my third visit he fires me. On my *third* visit!

He is angry and looks very, very scared.

This is Greece, I tell myself, this is a new decade. But it's really only Vegas + 10 = 1958.

My adventures in Greece had one happy outcome. I wrote a critical article about German romanticism's deadening nineteenth-century hold on Greek theatre. Published in *Drama Critic*, it resulted in an invitation to join the theatre department of Mercy College in Detroit, Michigan.

Years later fiction emerged from that experience. I ascribed those destabilizing undercurrents to Emily, who never actually existed, but who dreamlike walked those hot streets to the doctor's office, and finally to his apartment past the hair salon where lemon-sugar balls were used as depilatory:

AFTERNOON IN ATHENS

Her skin was as dry as her mouth, her feet felt scorched and swollen. She wore no hat and occasionally took shelter under a motionless canopy. She moved rigidly, her starched sleeveless dress standing away from her bare legs as if it wished no contact with her body. From time to time she stopped, staring at the corner building a block ahead, a sleepwalker drawn to a familiar landmark.

Each isolated sound — the grinding of a distant truck, a dog's bark, and now the staccato of her own high heels — made her feel more alone. With the shops closed and the vendors gone, the streets lost their smell and gave off the airless scent of a sealed attic on a summer day.

She remembered the attic and Clifford and the suffocating heat that stuck their bodies to each other like leeches. She kept saying no more and let me go and this isn't right and remember what we are to each other and God will punish us and remember, please remember. But she didn't let him go. She took more and gave more and thought to hell with everything, especially God.

Now here she was doing it all over again, not with her brother in the attic of their family cabin (Jesus those trusting parents and grandparents), no, not with any son of a bitch she could trust as she had trusted Clifford who had arranged for the abortion, kept everything quiet so they could carry on from where they'd left off, through her marriage to Bob and later to Andrew. No, here she was doing it all over again with this sly bastard who lived at the corner of Dionysius and Monika Streets.

Christalmighty, the giver of the grape and the giver of the son. When she told Niko how queer the whole thing was — his address, and the way the gods and the saints had fucked everything up — he lit a cigarette. For God's sake, you American women. Canadian, she corrected. He shrugged. She supposed that was the truth about the gods and the saints.

For God's sake most of the women she knew would never take their medals off their necks, not even when they jumped into bed with a louse who wasn't their husband. She even remembered that she had jumped out of bed one time to kneel down and say her prayers before jumping back in again and falling asleep. And always when she left Niko, if the church on the square was open, she'd go in and light a candle and stay for what seemed like hours just thinking over and over, O Jesus, O God, how I wish I loved you like I love that sonofabitch Niko or those other sonsofbitches. For Jesus' sake, for God's sake, for my sake, why do you lead me into temptation when you're supposed to lead me from it. And why do all those sonsofbitches teach me to love?

Dr. Nikos Kassimate was no ordinary man, but neither were Clifford nor Bob nor Andrew nor any of the others, the nameless ones that riffled through her memory like expertly shuffled cards. No, Clifford was an economist. He fulfilled his early promise, just as the family predicted. He was sent out on government missions and ran for public office and sometimes won. Robert inherited his father's furniture chain and gave her a generous settlement when they were divorced. Andrew owned stables full of beautiful horses. And the others, all the others did things, got places, were somebodies. Why was that?

How come they all knew who they were, while she had no idea who she was unless she were in love. Yes, when she was loving someone she knew who she was. She was Emily Henry, Emily who was radiant, Emily who was charming, Emily who was clever. She was not "Dr. Henry's little girl" anymore — how could she be now that she was in her thirties and he was dead? — nor Elizabeth Henry's bright daughter, the youngest of four bright daughters who might have all grown up to be just like their brilliant book-writing mother long since sequestered in a psychiatric institution. Those other three daughters had entered the religious life, while Emily's own brightness was dimmed by a series of overseas desk jobs with the Ministry of Foreign Affairs.

No, Emily in love knew who she was. In love she was walking uphill to Niko's apartment.

* * * * *

The embassy gave a cocktail party for a UN medical team en route to Cyprus or Africa or somewhere, and Niko was among the local doctors invited. Their hands met reaching for a drink. Emily felt no rush to withdraw from the touch. On the contrary. She threw her head back and laughed and held on. He said, I need that hand for surgery and laughed, too. I'll be careful, she told him. They left the party early.

He was witty and slightly vulgar. The hands were sensitive; the manners rough. She liked his long fingers and sharp tongue. He was different, not smooth like the aging men she usually dated.

He was no ordinary man. Niko was not merely a family doctor as her father had been. Niko was a surgeon. He was important. He was her lover. Had been for almost a year — fall, winter, and spring. No, not so much the spring, but the fall and winter. Then they were almost always alone. She cooked for him at her place. Sometimes they went to the Herod Atticus to concerts or to see the last of the season's plays.

His friends when she met them seemed to like her. She invited them to eat and drink at her apartment in Kiffizia and they always accepted.

"Ai!" Niko said, "you're pretty popular. Just keep the whiskey flowing. My friends are crazy about your scotch."

"And my cooking, too?"

He patted her rump. "You're not Greek."

Emily made sure to keep the whiskey flowing, but after a few parties her landlord complained of the noise so she took to visiting Niko's place at night or at any free time during the day or during their off hours. Their heaving bodies found space on his creaking bed or the worn wood floor. His landlord didn't complain about the noise.

But most of Niko's friends were married, and in the winter evenings Niko and Emily had more time alone. Actually Niko was married, too, at least officially, legally. His wife lived in Piraeus with the left-wing crowd.

"She is a bad painter but a good whore," Niko shrugged. "I pay her bills."

When spring came, Athens moved out-of-doors again. Niko's old friends were surprised to see Emily.

"O you're still with Niko; how nice."

That seemed odd to Emily. She thought it should be obvious that she and Niko belonged to each other. Surely everyone can see that our devotion is deep. Of course it isn't sensible for us to live under the same roof — our positions and the possibility of scandal, Niko says. Still, the Greeks are a sophisticated people; they should understand that we're inseparable.

Yet his friends were not quite comfortable with her. When she spoke they smiled indulgently and switched back to Greek. Niko signalled her to keep quiet.

As the weather grew warmer Emily drove Niko to Glyfada so they could eat by themselves. She chose a waterfront taverna where the tables straddled the sea and their sandalled bare feet could play games in it. But after a few visits, though he didn't object, he didn't play either.

Trips to tavernas became less frequent. Niko complained that he didn't have time to drive to the sea. Instead he met his friends at the cafes in Athens. There they met late at night when they were assured of coolness and a certain male solitude. The men were from Crete like Niko, understood each other's raucousness, sang and danced together, belched out their jokes and wry wisdom — women, good ones, bad ones, wives and others.

"A man wants a son to carry on his name."

"A guy like you, Niko, with such a good family in Crete, should get a strong woman of child-bearing age."

Very few women except inquisitive tourists sat at those tables after sunset. But sometimes Emily managed to find Niko and tried to join his crowd.

"Go," he told her. "You're embarrassing me."

She confined her visits to his apartment.

But his apartment smelled. All the apartments in Athens smelled. The plumbing was bad and the kitchens had the rank odour that old ice-boxes give off in the heat. Niko's apartment was in the rear of the building facing the courtyard. Retsina and aged meat stank up the hallways, stretching out to the treeless courtyard. The night air didn't blow it away but only blanketed the rooms more heavily with its staleness.

She said to Niko, "Come to the sea, all you Greeks love the sea."

That's how they came to drive out to Piraeus. He didn't want to go to Glyfada or to places near Sunion. He didn't want to be seen with her any longer. Or maybe he just wanted to go to Piraeus. Maybe he wanted to see that wife of his who was such a bad painter.

Most of the waters around the port were banned to swimmers. But the Greeks swam in them anyway. Niko and Emily found a cheap place that was on the water, but Niko grumbled, "Even cheap fish is too expensive for a Greek."

"Let me be host." Before they got out of the car she tried to slip him money.

He brushed her hand aside. "I'm not a whore," he said.

So Emily paid her own way each time they went.

After they ate they would walk down the rocky beach and go bathing. Niko liked to swim. He swam well and far out into the night. Isabel would try to follow him but she was scared. Why am I scared, she wondered. It would be nice to follow him and drown with him.

One night he'd been late getting home from the hospital. He said he wanted to stay in his apartment to rest, to study, to be alone. They quarrelled. But finally, sullenly, he agreed to go with her.

As they waded into the black water she thought I must follow him tonight, all the way out. Down, down, down, she said in time to each stroke. I should have pulled Clifford down. Should have but was too scared. She kept swimming. When she caught him, she grabbed his shoulder and said I'm tired. He told her to swim back to shore but she put both arms around his neck and pulled him under. He pushed himself away from her and when she came to the surface, he grabbed her hair.

"You bitch, you hysterical bitch, swim back to shore."

So she did.

It was clear she should have gone under. All her life she had wanted to go down. Under. But she kept swimming back, coming back. No one let her have things her own way. She wanted under, down, but here she was back on shore against her will, against her wishes. She sat on the jagged rocks. Her lungs hurt.

Her feet were bleeding.

"Christ," she said.

When Nikos came out of the water he muttered, "I don't want to go back to Athens with you."

"You can't stay here all night."

"Leave me at Spyro's cafe in Piraeus."

When they reached the cafe she said she was sorry. She begged him, "Forgive me, please come back with me."

"No."

She threw herself across him and held on to the car door.

"For God's sake! You women! Shit!"

Emily drove to Athens alone.

She didn't call him and she didn't go to see him. I'll give him the cold shoulder for a while, it always works. But she wondered if it would, because as she thought back over it she remembered that sometimes it didn't. Then one night she called him on the phone but there was no answer. She went over to his apartment and sat on the top step outside the door but he never came back. At dawn she showered and dressed for work. She called the hospital in the morning. She was told he was in surgery. She drove to his place at dusk. Reluctantly he let her in. He was shaving and went back to the bathroom to finish.

"Niko, where are you going?"

He said, "We're not married, don't nag, don't pry, don't make any more scenes."

"But where are you going?"

"On a call."

"Where?"

"I'm a doctor. I'm going on a call."

"May I go with you?"

"No."

"I did, I used to, I went with my father and sat in the car and waited for him."

"Well I'm not your father and you won't go with me."

"Where are you going? Are you going to Piraeus to see your wife?"

"That is none of your business."

"*I'm* a good whore!" said Emily Henry.

"Yes," said Dr. Nikolas Kassimate. "But not a bad painter, so go without making a scene."

* * * * *

With the shops closed and the vendors gone, the streets lost their smell, unless it was the airless smell of a sealed attic on a stifling summer day. She saw the air tremble with heat. She said to herself I am Dr. and Mrs. Henry's bright daughter Emily, and I will walk into the apartment house at the corner of Dionysius and Monika Streets and up the four flights to Niko's flat.

The End

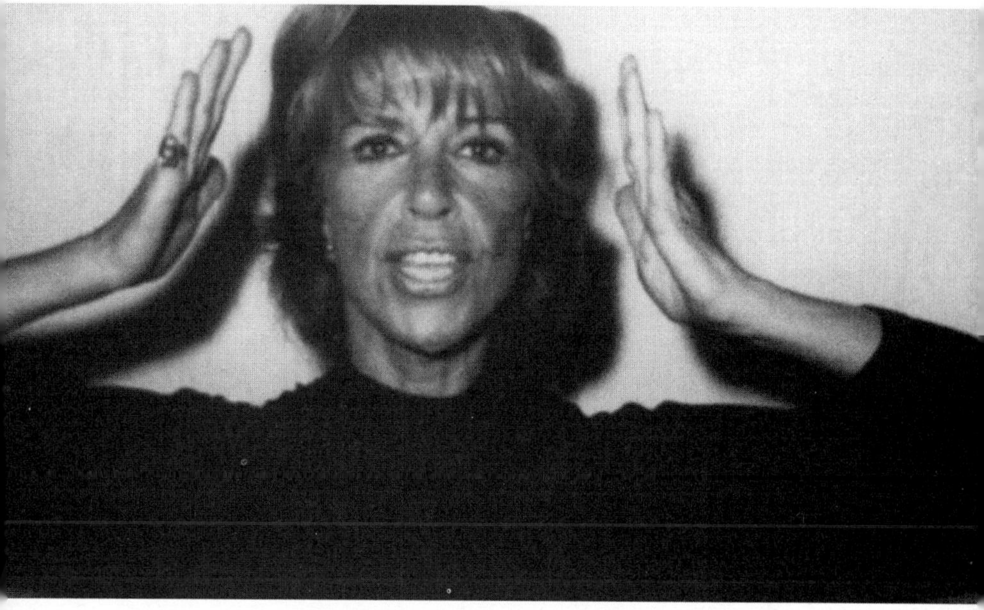

Gladys and Harold

I MET GLADYS ON A CARIBBEAN cruise in the 1960s.

But first I met her husband Harold. Our deck chairs were next to each other's. I saw he was reading a book about Teilhard de Chardin, the paleontologist. Mutual admiration for the Jesuit made our exchange of names less formal: Please call me Harold.

I had the impression that Harold was a gentleman, perhaps a scholar. I found out later that he also owned a factory reputed to make the finest costume jewellery in the United States.

The ship's steady roll almost lulled me to sleep under the late afternoon sun. Remotely I heard my friendly neighbour whisper, "It's cocktail time; I'm taking off to find my wife — either in the pool or the gym or ... " As he left I pulled my beat-up beach hat over my eyes and yielded to silent forgetfulness. My thoughtful brother had sent me on this cruise to recuperate from the sturm and drang of work overload and collapsing marriage. Yes. So shhh ... blessed silence, aimless drifting, empty space, peace over troubled waters ... CRASH!

I sat up violently. What comet had jarred my planet? Beside my deck chair a ton of metal lay collapsed, jingling, snorting. Snorting? *Speaking*. O my God! No, that's her line:

"My God have you seen my husband?" The voice emerged from a swamp of silver, gold, and sparkling pieces of rock. It was definitely a woman's voice, a bit nasal, not indelicate, a sort of potpourri of idioms, accents, intonations; garnered souvenirs of world travel.

"Are you Mrs. — "

"Sorry dear, should introduce myself. I'm Gladys, Harold's wife. Call me Glad." Slowly, a body extricated itself from dangling bracelets, earrings, necklaces, ankle chains and fully-ringed fingers. It managed to stand. Upright. I leaned forward as if to help.

Incroyable! This was a living skeleton, breathing, talking. I could make out eyes surrounded by mink lashes, one for the upper lids, one for the lower, and a rainbow of contoured shades of green, blue, and violet. Capped teeth blazed white behind lips glossed red enough to flash night signals to passing planes.

This was the gentleman's wife?

Shielding my eyes, I frowned accusingly, "Your husband has been looking for you."

"I'm not easy to find."

"He mentioned the pool, the gym, something about cocktails."

"Poor darling" — she sounded as if she meant it — "he can't ... or won't ... remember that I have my body massage first." She patted her concave stomach. I looked at her overbleached hair and skin-stretched face and recognized her in an instant. This was the woman I'd overheard other wives bitching about:

– That revolting woman.
– Married to that nice gentleman.
– She's disgusting. Did you see the pass she made at Charles?
– She made a pass for Tommy, too.
– She'd make a pass at any man standing. Or floating.
– New York whore.
– Jew bitch.
– They're all the same.
– Doesn't fool me with those French phrases she tosses even at the French waiters. Makes me *faire un renvoi.*
– What?
– Belch, dear.
– What does she hope to accomplish in those slinky bare-assed dresses?
– Anorexic.
– You'd be skinny too if you'd been around the block as often as she has.

– I told Tommy to ignore her.
– Did he?
– He does now. I told him he could straighten up as much as he likes but if he flies he flies with *me*. Or I'll ground him for good.
– They're all the same.

* * * * *

The sun sinking, a slight breeze ruffling the empty deck chairs, hardly anyone around now but Glad and me. Just a little while ago she'd said, I'm not easy to find. She's mistaken. The theatricality, the exhibitionism are a plea for attention. I want to protect her.

"Glad," I smile, "are-you-or-have-you-ever-been a dancer, or on the stage?"

She laughs, surprised; "Yes and yes. And you?"

"I'm a newly-born Canadian; we don't have the Fifth." McCarthy memories make me nervous, but I answer, "Yes."

Glad slaps on her bathing cap, unloads her bangles. "Let's go for a swim. Let's *talk*!"

We flaunt our Australian crawls, gossip over our backstrokes. Instant sisters. Add water and mix: where we'd trained, performed (she with the Metropolitan Opera Ballet), to whom we were or had been married, number of children if any, and, winkingly, lovers current (any names to drop?).

"Well, I'm living a different way of life these last few years."

"Oh?"

"I'm a Catholic."

"But I know *lots* of them!"

"But I decided to take it seriously."

"I sometimes wish I could take religion seriously." She folds forward, treads water. I do, too. Despite her waterproof mascara, tears slide from between those lashes. "My husband," she gasps, "Harold. He's so good … so fine … actually a wonderful person" — she flails her arms — "but nothing

I do, nothing" — she swallows a mouthful of pool — "sex zilch, nothing works, I've tried everything, *every*-thing."

She crawls toward the diving board. I float, think about those tears, watch one or two laggards leave the pool as the dinner gong chimes.

Harold appears, doffs his cap, leans over the deep end, "Oh Glad, *here you are*! I've been looking everywhere. You've found a friend!"

* * * * *

Late dinner, late drinks, and of course late, late dancing. We sit at one of those tiny tables scattered around dance floors. He sips an old-fashioned, I, at his invitation, a scotch.

"That's Glad's favourite, too," he beams. "She's disciplined, her ballet training you know, never has more than two, stays in perfect shape, takes care of her figure."

* * * * *

Insistent drum, drum, drumming. Dance tunes, itching feet, pressing bodies. Ravel's Bolero, of course, couples shuffling toward the dance floor, two-by-two in Noahed memory; beat, beat, beat. Like metronomes. Glad's head on Harold's shoulder, pelvis grinds as the orchestra whines to silence before blowing out an unexpected blast of "Begin the Beguine." The knowledgeable movers pick up the rhythm. One is at hand, lithe, sunburned. He cuts in and Harold returns to our table.

We both watch her glide into the arms of her advancing partner who makes sure his grip pulls her toward him for the first flourish. The Beguine begins.

I think Harold likes to watch.

Lights rotate, alternate bastard pink with amber, flood over the couples who can't take their eyes off Glad, nor her partner around whom she wraps one leg with a kick to rival a Rockette's. They dip, she arches her back, the band vocalist catches his breath and somewhere between a whistle and a whisper sings, "Let them begin the beguine ... make them play ... "

The lights seem to gather into one tight spot on the duet. Other couples, annoyed and angrily repressing their fury, leave what has turned out to be a professional display. Exhibition. Invasion.

Harold presses his cold drink to his face. "Women are jealous of her, don't know what an angel she is."

I look at her face coming up from a sensational lunge. For a split second the spot focuses on her eyes, desperate eyes, the eyes of a child, terrified, pleading for a hideaway.

Harold applauds; the orchestra strikes up a faster number, people return to the dance floor. This will be the last dance. The langorous tenor sings, "That old black magic has me in its spell ... that you weave so well ... the mate that fate had me created for ... " Harold murmurs as if to himself, but I can hear him, "O those friends of hers, bitches, they use her," he smiles, "and she never says a mumbling word." I'm struck by his using the words of a black spiritual. His eyes never leave Glad's dancing. "The phone calls for fundraisers for the Country Club, like a whole goddam review!"

"Excuse me ... "

Harold sips at his drink, stares at his black magic. "They couldn't care less about the hours she spends with handicapped children; she gets those kids to clap, jump, skip. I've seen them. And no one knows that she takes night courses at the university; Shakespeare, art history, always trying to make up for lost time."

And the song goes on: "Then darling down down down I go ... round and round I go ... "

* * * * *

I never met Harold again, but Glad became a godsend ... that "Jew bitch," always seeking reality, always grasping any scrap of truth dropped or flung her way, said goodbye as the cruise ended with one last bump at the New York dock. Glad promised to keep in touch. But they all say that (they're all the same!) after picking my brains: tell me about where you live, what you *DO*, *believe*, how interesting, even *exciting*, I mean a woman with your background pulling up stakes and moving to a rented house in a small Michigan town to teach NUNS and PRIESTS and young students and not just CATHOLIC ones, for what? O! because you *believe*, because you're exploring because Hey keep in touch 'cause I may come up for the summer course do you accept people like me meaning non-Catholics meaning Jews — yes I smile if you are seriously interested in applying your talents and training for a while. How long? A few weeks a few months some years. And tell me she questions with a final hug, Why did you steer me away from those women on shipboard, tell me to avoid speaking to them? No Glad let it go. O please. O no. And I never did. Never.

To our surprise she did arrive, worked days, nights, practising speech exercises, making feeble attempts to sing, her voice becoming sweeter more assured as she created pre-classic, then classic, then modern dance forms, speaking, singing, moving simultaneously, dove into plays and characters, was heard not merely mouthing Shakespeare but experiencing *The Dark Lady Within*.

With the same discipline she walked daily to the nearby village, where to her shock she discovered the grocer did NOT carry Beluga caviar — or any caviar for that matter — and like a little girl her long ballet legs swiftly erased the five-mile return trip to the studio. There she announced the party she'd planned for us had to make do with dips and cheese, but the others loved her anyway, relieved to avoid tasting, probably swallowing, the foreign *yes Russian* stuff.

Glad became one of us in the States, in Canada, first piecemeal, then with her husband's tolerant cooperation the longer training periods evolved into tours in the U.S. and Canada, and longer periods where spiritual sparks ignited genuine interest and then love for Christ. Timidly she reached for a God she longed to touch, a holiness she didn't realize she already embodied in her generosity and sensitivity.

There was Father Peter at our studio in the Ottawa Valley; actually he lived a few hundred yards from The Moving Word Centre, the name that emerged for our ministry as we remodelled our one-room schoolhouse, dug our heels into planning, preparing, praying for the unknown adventure with students from both sides of Canada, England, Italy, the United States, and Peru! So Glad moved in a cosmopolitan, even catholic world, balanced among the ambitiously theatrical, the academically curious, and the genuinely passionate creative — a world not unfamiliar to her but for that peculiar twist, a spiritual spin different from any circle bourgeois or bohemian in which she'd ever made the rondes.

The atmosphere for Glad was the associating of a performer's blood sweat and tears with the enlightening intimacy of pure God and pure Man personified by our priest Father Peter Nearing. The first pure father she'd ever known. Just as she'd told me on our first swim together on shipboard, she'd "tried everything" with the husband she truly loved but all she'd learned at the hands of her natural father was from the titillating visits he engineered to whorehouses so she could view and absorb the finer arts of sex. She adored her father, he was such a successful speculator, such a good provider for her wonderful English mother, so gentle, so refined, so good.

Child abuse was not then a viable currency.

How right Bishop Brietenbach was to give me
a good hard slap when he pronounced my Confirmation
name, "Mary Magdelene" (then smiled reassuringly). How
was he to know that this pert young woman so charmingly
dressed for the occasion would in a few years' time whole-
heartedly embrace chastity, that the crowded Detroit
cathedral would dissolve into a bare sweet one-room

Canadian schoolhouse along a fast-flowing country river? How was he to know, or indeed how was I to know that I'd be writing lyrics with those very words for a modest prize-winning film to my loyal partner Paul's music?

"How were we to know, nobody ever told us, no, nobody ever told us, long and long ago."

Or that one evening when darling Glad sat with us in the little studio and saw "Catherine's Song" and watched my frenetic conversion story unreel that the two of us would glimpse the real Mary Magdelene, and in some measure celebrate that woman's ascendancy spiral however haltingly toward the living Christ.

Alleluia, Christ is risen!

The curtain was drawn when Glad died a prolonged death from cancer.

Before she reached heights visible to us, I had the privilege of writing and choreographing a short film for her, *Alpha and Omega*.

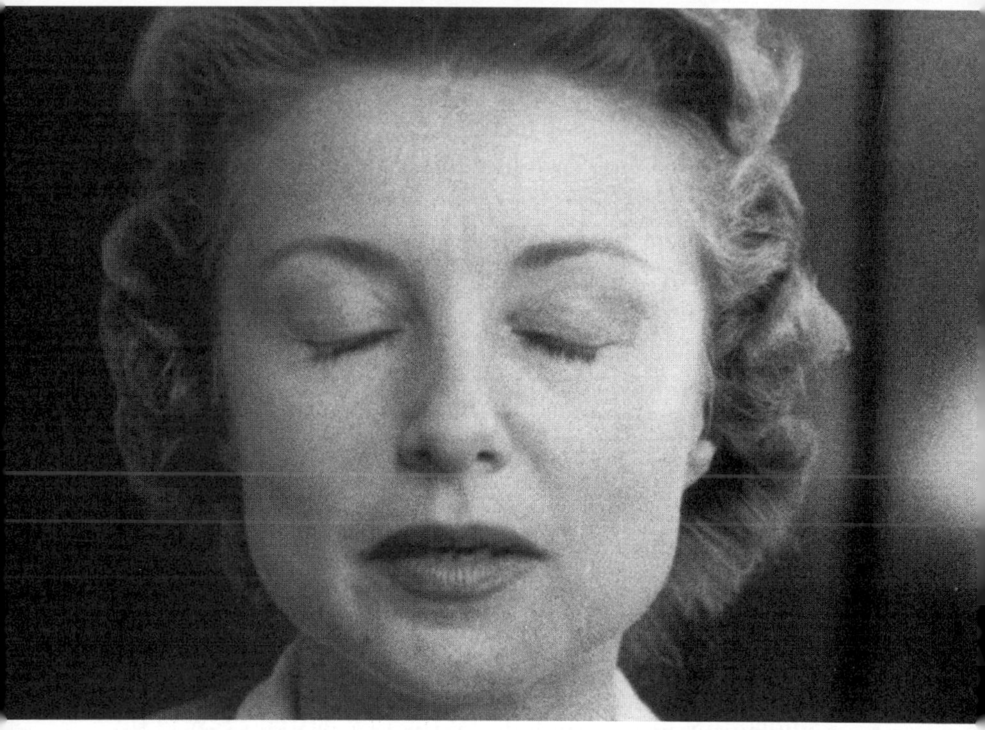

Split

YUGOSLAVIA WAS NOT A COUNTRY I'D HAVE CHOSEN but it was cheap. And I was tired. I didn't know a lot about it; I don't think many people did in 1976. I was in Italy anyway, on a sabbatical from teaching theatre, so it was simple: I boarded ship at Pescara and sailed to Split. The brochures presented Yugoslavia as fabled and picturesque; I added dramatic — perfect for a busman's holiday. I could sketch my heart out with ideas for set designs and costumes.

My hopes were bouyant. So was the Adriatic. The afternoon glowed with that special blue associated with my ship's namesake, Tintoretto.

I stood on deck taking in the whole view. As I turned a pair of eyes stopped me. There he sat, a man in his prime, perhaps forty-nine or fifty. His face was bearded, his head shaved, his right arm amputated below the shoulder. A woman was with him. She was tall, straight, her spine not bending even when she leaned over to listen to him speak; her Slavic face, structured in sharp planes, impassive, relieved only by a faint smile when she answered him. She stood by his deck chair — at his elbow if his elbow had been there.

I smiled first at the woman, but the raw hatred I saw in the man's steel-grey eyes forced me to lower my own before smiling at him. I cannot say why, but I felt compelled to persuade him that I was not merely a tourist come to bargain or cheat, but a friendly foreigner eager to learn about and admire his country. It seemed terribly important to win him to my side.

My side? On what side had he left his arm? In the Resistance? The Civil War? Fascist? Communist? Was he Croat? Serb? Muslim? Christian? Is he — had he ever been — an enemy? Had he lost not only his arm in some violence, but all hope as well? What is that to me? Or me to it? Why should he focus such hatred on me? Was my imagination playing tricks? I raised my eyes again. There was nothing but his eyes, unblinking tombs of gun-metal grey that erased all other features. I was looking into hell.

I heard a voice. It was mine speaking to the woman beside him. I was babbling in a mixture of English, French, and a few Italian phrases. Did she know of a pleasant pension … ? What about bus routes to … ? Train connections from … ? Inanities. His military bearing cast a shadow between us. I noticed her broad-knuckled hands when she turned up his collar.

The woman answered in halting English, her brown eyes darting chameleon-like from me to him and back again. I heard only disjointed words separated from sense because of the pounding in my ears.

I turned in the direction of the ship's stern and made my way below.

Wherever I went the man's eyes bored into my back. In the passageways his shadow blocked the light from the portholes. If I abruptly stopped in the hope of embarrassing him, he never wavered. His eyes pinned me against a wall here, a door there.

I took to my cabin directly after dinner, barricaded the locked doors with my luggage and turned out all the lights except the blue night lamp. My porthole faced the lulling Adriatic, but I saw the eyes of the amputated man staring through its curtained windows. I felt the stab of something more than hatred.

The nightmare began, a series of frightening clip-shots:

> My feet grope for a foothold but the
> pebbles and stones give way. I dig my
> fingernails into the dirt, but it,
> too, offers no purchase. The rock is
> beyond my reach. I try to peer into
> the blackness but I keep slipping,
> sliding. I crouch, cling to the dirt.
> It slithers through my fingers, my
> toes. It is no good stretching for
> that bush, trying to get a grip at its
> root. I feel it is no good. Useless.

I clench my teeth, hold my breath in a
spasm of hopeless fear. An avalanche
covers me — rocks, dirt, thorned
branches — but now they are not falling
over me, they are falling beneath me.
I am powerless in black space. I
cannot save myself. My eyes are open
in blind blackness. I grope through
space, my feet touch nothing, nothing.
My fingertips hit, strike. Black ice.
The phone rings. I lift the receiver.
There is no sound. I speak. There is
no sound coming from my throat. I try
to place the receiver in its holder
but my hand is frozen to dry ice and
the phone is still ringing. How can it
be when the receiver is off the hook?
But I am the receiver and I am not off
the hook.
WHERE ARE ALL THOSE DOCUMENTS?
THE PASSPORT AND THE FILES?

I can't remember. Whenever I leave
the studio, I can't remember its name
or address. I can't find my way back.
It has Latin letters above its portal.
I can't read Latin, but I know those
letters mean "terra cotta," terror
caught her.
When I come up from the subway, I look
both ways to find where to go. There
is a man following me. He offers
directions. I know it before he says it.
I turn left, put my hands in my pockets
and grasp the paintbrushes tightly, so
tightly they break. But I cling to

them. It is raining heavily and as I paddle along the puddled streets, I hear the man's black oilskin slicker flapping behind me. I am lost again but I need new paintbrushes. I go into a store. There is only one counter. It is stacked high with newspapers. The black headline *HiTlErStAlIn Takes Madrid* covers the entire front page. The newspaper is heavy. I try to take it, but the hooded clerk wearing jet black eyeglasses places his long-nailed dirt-encrusted finger on the newspaper stack, shakes his head, says they are not for sale, they are "premature." It doesn't matter, I tell him. I can see through the papers, they are transparent. Just give me the paintbrushes. He points to a silver menorah from which seven sable brushes hang on brass rings, and says they are for sale. The man who has been following me says, "You will pay for it." I don't know if he is speaking to me or to the clerk. I take a drachma from my pocket and murmur, "Of course." The clerk reaches under the counter for a *Deutsche Mark* in which to wrap my brushes. Just as I take them, flashbulbs pop and a black phone, frozen to my hand, rings rings rings.

There was a faint drizzle the next morning. I thought I'd circle the deck a few times before coffee. I tried to keep pace with other passengers, half-jogging to match my small steps to their longer strides.

As I began my third lap, there was an increasing sea swell. Drizzle became downpour. The other passengers vanished below deck. I held back for one last breath of the salt air, then made a dash for the door.

It would not open. I pulled at the knob. I tried to hold it in the whipping wind, but kept sliding on the deck. I pushed and pulled. The door opened. The man stood there staring with his steely eyes, then disappeared into a nearby doorway.

That evening, the bustle and excitement of docking preoccupied me, although I was puzzled when a brash young taxi driver grabbed my luggage and rushed me through the crowd as if I were a visiting VIP. With a big smile and a few words of English he made it clear that he would take me to a good pension, "clean, cheap, good, good." I looked through the taxi's rear window to the stalled Customs line. No one else had been released.

There was a great grinding of brakes. Jarring springs mingled their racket with the intermittent shouts of the driver, "Not worry, not worry." Against my exhausted protests, he sped farther away from the city lights. He drove, he careened, he roared over endless dark roads in a blackish haze. We crashed from one place to another only to be told by the driver, "No vacant." Hour after hour we hurtled forward in blindness. The driver no longer bothered to shout at me over his shoulder, nor did he permit me to get out of the car at any of his aborted stops. At midnight we finally halted in front of a huge white building. Isolated in the moonlight, it looked like a grounded ghost ship. Its doors opened the moment the taxi stopped. We had been expected.

Two people stood framed in the lighted hall, a short burly man about my own height, wearing a long white jacket much like a doctor's coat, and a rather large woman whose dress had the appearance of a summer military uniform. They grinned as we stepped inside, spoke rapidly to the driver, ushered him out, and closed the door.

They led me along a painfully bright hallway to an unwindowed room piled with crates shrouded in khaki-coloured canvas. There was a bar in one corner with a half-dozen liquor bottles, one opened. Two shot glasses were next to it.

The man pointed to himself. "Tito." He laughed, mocking the dead Resistance leader's militant expression. "And Svetlana." He laughed again, jabbing the woman with his elbow. I pantomimed the need for sleep. He pointed to the shot glasses which Svetlana filled, handing one to me. I shook my head and remembered a long-forgotten Russian "*Nyet.*" I bent to pick up my suitcase, spilling the drink. Tito's foot pushed my luggage to the wall. Svetlana clucked oh-ohs. I straightened and looked directly at the man. For the first time I noticed that his left eye was glass.

"Room," I said. "Room."

Svetlana took the lead. I straggled behind her, trailing my suitcase as best I could to an alcove three-quarters filled by a garishly covered bed. On a rickety table stood an unshaded lamp. The space, like the house, looked unused, unlived in.

I turned to the woman, waiting for her to leave. She held out her hand. "Money." I reached into my purse for my passport and a roll of bills. She tossed the passport on the bed, and before I could count out my dollars, she grabbed a fistful.

"Also taxi," she said, and still smiling, sauntered back along the hallway.

Distant doors slammed shut, clanged and echoed through the empty building. I dropped to the bed. I decided not to undress. I left the ugly little light on. It flickered as a motorcycle snarled to life outside. I closed my eyes, but the unshaded bulb kept flickering, winking.

> Flashbulbs keep exploding in that Italian
> restaurant in the Piazza Navona.
> "Does that still frighten you?" he asks.
> Not understanding him — after all, I am
> no celebrity — but wanting to please, I
> answer, "Yes, yes, noise frightens me,

ever since the war." (But that isn't
true. I have always been terrified of
unusual sounds; sleep never comes easily
and sleep is never sound.)

His knowing Irish eyes lower to the
elaborate menu. He smiles, motions to
the server (is she really a waitress?)
who solemnly pours wine into my glass.
"Water for me," he says, the white
Dominican sleeve sliding over his slack
wrist. He clicks his glass against mine.
"Now tell me why you *really* came to
Italy."

Alarms and excursions! Messerschmitts
dive and phones keep ringing. No voices
but a humming, humming. The mean
little planes pierce the night sky, come
down, down, down toward our trench.
Isn't it beautiful — the ack-ack, the
tracers, the explosions? I snuggle deep
in the uniformed arm of my English colonel.
If I prick the bloated belly of the dead
German soldier, will it explode? I look
at him and laugh; his eyes follow me. He
wants to be painted, he wants to be
remembered. I'm the artist who can do it.
In red, black, and white. If I could
just shoot him. "Why the camera?" asks
the priest, and I tell him I remember!

That's why I've returned to Italy. To
sleep, to dream, perchance to die
remembering.

A steady, staring light shone from a high slat near the ceiling, not moonlight, but a piercing beam directed toward my eyes. I tried to twist away from its glare, covered my eyes with my arm, wiped the sweat and tears from my face. I lay still, powerless to cry out in this shroud of silence.

The first streaks of dawn washed out the last traces of the torchlight. Before the sun shone, I made the decision to return to Italy.

The building was empty, every door unlocked as if my escape had been anticipated. In rumpled clothes, suitcase in hand, I trudged deserted unpaved roads searching for someone, anyone, who could give me directions back to the port of embarkation. The sun rose, promising a day of sweltering disquiet. And still I saw no people, no vehicles of any kind. Finally, hungry and thirsty, I sat down by a muddy stream and cooled my hands and feet. The glare was too intense to see anything beyond a few scrub bushes that marked a fork in the road.

I looked at the scene; a bare circle of twigs and pebbles. Hovering over it, a pall of fear, a jumble of fragmented images, a sense of emptiness, desolation. I wanted to remember it, all that went into its making. I needed to sketch, to forget nothing. My pen rushed over my sketch pad trying to capture the dryness, the texture of desert in the middle of nowhere.

Tents, helmets, canteens spilled over the paper. I closed my eyes for a moment's respite. When I opened them and looked at the drawings, I saw amputated arms holding back tent flaps, lifting canteens, pressing helmets down on ravaged heads where eyes hollowed with hatred stared back at me. Here was war, the alpha and omega, all of it captured for me to flesh out, find a stage large enough to encompass it. Before I closed the book, I touched my sketches gently as if fingering precious fabrics.

I heard the rumble of a truck. It stopped before I flagged it.

"Boat?" the woman driver called above the racing motor.

The woman let me off at the port office. I lugged my suitcase down. She didn't return my waved goodbye. Instead she peered sharply from right to left, then, bending low over the steering wheel, she looked straight into my eyes. She thrust two forked fingers at me smartly, repeatedly, and drove away. She was not smiling.

Insigniaed officials checked and stamped my documents, this time in the usual way. I headed for the Tintoretto's gangplank with the other jostling passengers. As I reached the rail, I turned to look behind me.

In the shadow of the Customs shed, a dim work-light hung above the long information counter. From behind it two piercing eyes were turned in my direction. The man with the amputated arm stood immobile. His penetrating eyes bore into mine. Next to him, almost in darkness, a woman smiled. What woman? From the ship? From the house where I'd stayed? The truck driver?

The line of passengers moved forward and I was forced to go with them. After we'd sailed I discovered that I'd lost my sketch pad.

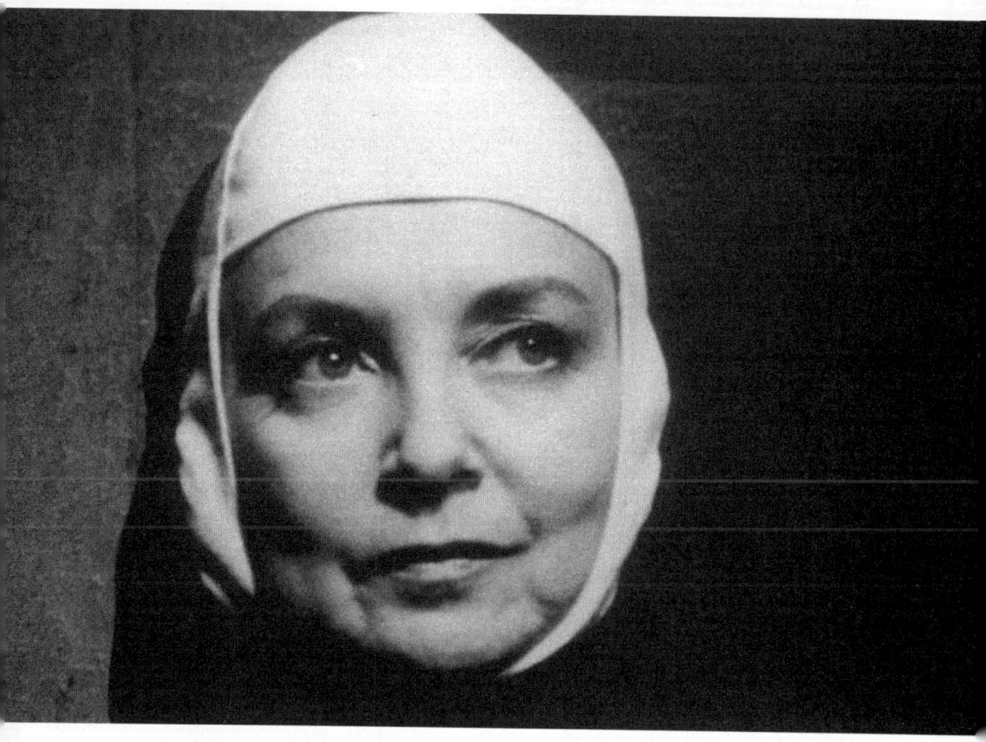

There She Stands

DECEMBER 1966. In the woods of Eastern Ontario:
It was almost twilight; the snaky snow-covered highway gave on to a country road silhouetted against the grey-white sky overhung with black branches. Our driver leaned wearily over the wheel. "Thank God, we're here."

Silence. We looked at each other. "Here?"

A void. Then a tiny sound, the softest bell followed by a rush of the sweetest series of bells joining each other. A deep strong woman's voice called, "Welcome!" We jumped from the car to see the woman of the bells. There she stood, every inch of her Russian girth beaming with greeting. The B. — Baroness long exiled, mistress of this icy hill.

I'd been invited by the B. to bring Choreologia to Combermere to conduct a workshop for her staff. I knew nothing of this community, but had been recommended by one of their associate members who'd studied with me. I'd brought along two members to perform with me.

In the little chapel above their dining room we began with excerpts from my plays, including the *Peace Prayer of St. Francis*. The chapel benches had been pushed to the sides to make room for our choreography. With Francis' closing lines — It is in dying that we are born to eternal life! — there was absolute quiet.

Then Catherine — the B. — walked slowly to me, bowed in that unforgettable Russian manner, and kissed my hands: This is what I've been begging my people to do, she said, respond with their *entire* being to God. Tell them, she gestured toward her group, ask them do they see, understand? There was a rustling as the stunned little audience leaned forward. Tell them what? I, too, needed spiritual alerting so I welcomed their questions:

- Well, to be honest, to concentrate on the *body* so much, what happens to my prayer life?
- Yes, for me it would split me wide open, detract from quiet meditation ...

– Actually (a man's voice) awareness of *your* body rather than the Body of our Lord could be a sort of temptation, maybe?
– Right, even hearing your own words rather than Jesus'. I mean, how do I sound ... look ... feel?
– And we're not dancers ...
– Or actors! (Polite but unanimous gentle laughter.)

The B. looks at me, shrugs, spreads her hands, and with that inimitable accent: See how afraid they are of their bodies. Tell them like you showed us, this body is God's gift.

OK, listen: I created Choreologia because I had to. Let's be honest. If you're among those who are satisfied with the statues and paintings and dripping decor — of St. Thérèse of Lisieux, "The Little Flower," for example—then Choreologia is not for you. But if you want to grow, extend beyond the literal meaning of words and stretch toward a glimpse of the infinite, where the community of saints are *not* confined, then perhaps Choreologia may be for you — it is a radical change from traditional religious dramatic forms. Not the answer, not the Way, but an arrow pointing in its direction. However, in the words of my script that we're going to be working on, *It's a risky thing passing over!*

Does your image of Thérèse Martin remain that of a little woman, a tiny girl actually, who entered cloistered convent life in Lisieux a healthy mischievous fifteen-year-old, was struck down almost immediately by consumption, lay prone coughing blood-stained sheets for eight years, listening only for God's word?

Yes, that is certainly acceptable and certainly an acceptable prayer. But then how is it possible for an active person, a creative person, to *perform* such a saint?

Thérèse has become alive for me. She can't remain like the statues, the paintings and stained-glass windows, hands piously clasped, stationary, immobile. Saints are not immobile, Christ is not immobile — the Holy Spirit *moves*. How might such *interior* action be incarnated, freed without fear? That is your question and mine.

As for me, when my body soul and spirit respond to Thérèse's confidence and love, her words do not merely merge or meld, but *fuse* and *burn* into a new canticle, my play, *The New Canticle*. And that *becomes* Choreologia!

The Blessed Mother, the big and little flowers (Teresa of Avila and Thérèse of Lisieux), Chiara (St. Clare of Assisi), Marie Guyart (Marie de l'Incarnation), St. Francis: all these whole/holy people spoke intimately, even idiomatically. And so infiltrated my dramatic treatment of Euripides' Jocasta, the dark lady sonnets of Shakespeare, liturgical prayers; indeed — the *Peace Prayer*.

* * * * *

In the warmth and confidence of private meetings through the following days with Catherine de Hueck Doherty — the B. — she embraced me and said, "You have an apostolate."

Heavy with Biblical connotations, that word had only vague meaning for me. An apostolate carried responsibilities. Was I to be sent away on a mission? Not by the B.'s community, that was made clear.

How could this be? I had an apostolate? And what would I do about it? I was, I thought, finally what I'd always wanted to be: a Christian theatre artist. Could an artist also be an apostle? There were lots of voices suggesting, advising, warning. But what was the still small voice within saying?

Several years earlier, at Catholic University, Dominic Rover O.P. wrote in his critique of *The New Canticle*, "Modern art is essentially a theological art, a religious art. Those who miss this point find themselves with great artistic weapons for the conquest — of nothingness. Sara Lee Stadelman has not missed the point; she stands in very fact upon it ... "

I choreographed Thérèse of Lisieux on the body and with the vocal strength and force of a contemporary young woman. I dared to have her solo downstage centre to the footlights and share her secret with the audience, whispering, "I want to be a saint!"

I dared that because that's what *I* really wanted to be — a whole and holy person; it's that passion I prayed to imbue in those I trained.

Thomas Merton's essay on the paintings of William Congdon justified my approach to Choreologia, confirmed my instincts about the *roots* of theatre, the *essence* of drama: "Abstract expressionism has been and remains a deeply spiritual protest." It had never been my intention to shock audiences. My break from conventional theatre forms was creative necessity, a protest against the centuries-old sentimentality in religious art. This demanded fresh beginnings. And that was the verb I was pursuing. Take for example Thérèse of Lisieux's death scene in *The New Canticle*. Traditionally such a scene would be portrayed piously. Yet Thérèse's blood sisters called her "little minx, little madcap." But Thérèse's verb obviously was not "to die," but *to rush to eternal life*:

Rush! ... Rush! ... Rush to the lowest place, not the highest!
Rush, rush, rush!

So ... as an artist I had to allow her to pursue that verb; I could not impose a sad, possibly sanctimonious, pall over her.

The New Canticle achieved not only an artistic breakthrough but the *pursuit of my verb*. The Calvinist conditioning of youth and hard-won Catholicism of maturity coalesced and informed my deepening faith. I broke from stereotyped forms and found a spiritual approach to both secular and religious themes. In Merton's words, "the *logos* set free." He saw that "the mere formalistic treatment of religious themes [is] not necessarily a glory either for art or religion."

In the wooden parlour on that wintry night when the B. said, "You have an apostolate," and pushed me out of her nest, I was a spiritual fledgling, I needed someone to teach me to fly.

I went back to my home in Detroit where only a few years before a vociferous minority infuriated by our production of *Teresa of Avila* wrote to *The Michigan Catholic*,

– *Imagine Teresa of Avila with Freudian complexes!*
– *If my daughter behaved like that I'd have her put away.*
– *A saint showing her ankles! Whatever can I report to my Altar Society?*

The Mother's Guild of Marygrove College, where I was teaching, had threatened to remove their daughters and to picket the college. The college President refused to budge; the mothers backed down.

Dorothy Day, the Catholic activist and iconoclast, supported my work. In one brief meeting she confirmed my objective to witness the living God in theatre and advised, "Decide whether you are a teacher or director — whether you stay with the institution or go it alone." I opted to go it alone as a director.

Another supporter was Father Clement Kern (actually Monsignor but title never used). "Mrs. Stadelman," he said publicly, "you're welcome to perform in my church *any*time." He was pastor of the beloved Most Holy Trinity parish in Detroit's Corktown. The upscaled Irish had moved away leaving room for disadvantaged Mexican families. Father Kern devoted himself to them. He responded with even-handed compassion to their daily needs, often absurd demands, pleas, sometimes threats, as he tried to resolve their tragic crises:

"*Padre*," an angry mother accuses, "you send my son Jesus Maria a *blanco-y-negra* television. He should have *colore* like that good-for-nothing Mrs. Hereras! — *Mrs!* — *Madre de Dios!*"

"The problem," Father Kern explains, "is the prison guards didn't like delivering even the black-and-white. Your Jesus is too *violente*."

A wino staggers in, bleary from either too much or not enough. "Need a pad, Father — few nights." Father offers his Ford, "the black one out front. Door's always open, make yourself comfortable. But clear out by nine in the morning, I have to go see the bishop."

The peeling walls of Most Holy Trinity parish house are decorated with the image of the Virgin of Guadalupe. The hallway leading to Father's office is lined with old church pews filled with penitents, mendicants, and middle-class professionals.

The little priest, silver-haired, gentle, almost handsome, his cigarette-burned cassock as bedraggled as the reformed porter who mans the door and the telephone, has to find a new place every day to hide the altar wine because Father refuses to lock his church; celebrates countless Mass requests and accepts no fee — none; finds time each day to pray the rosary with his parishioners, to work with labour unions, with city planners, to visit the police hospital, bless and reassure prisoners that he'll hold their personal property until their release, and still finds time to encourage an artist:

"You need a change of scene, a deeper, broader spirituality." He gave us one hundred dollars for two round-trip tickets to Mexico City. It was 1968! "Discover the Virgin of Guadalupe," he said, and sent me on my first mission as an apostle. In poverty. "Depend on Our Lady" — and on his letter introducing us to the Benedictine priests. So sure of its effect was I that I fell blissfully asleep before the Greyhound was up and running on the Michigan expressways.

* * * * *

February 1968. The Mexican border, eleven at night:
"Let's sit separately in the waiting room. I don't think it's wise for us to be seen travelling as a couple." I am pointedly

speaking quietly. Of course Paul asks why and his resonant voice even in a whisper can be heard the length and breadth of the border. But I am still an American citizen, Paul's passport is Canadian; I am married, he is not.

We sit apart and hang back in order to be interviewed last, so that if there are difficulties we won't be overheard.

An immaculately mustachioed Customs Officer signals to me. I go. He examines my passport. He signals Paul. He examines Paul's passport.

"You are not one-by-one. You are a couple." His black eyes flick from me to Paul; "*Bueno*," he says, and turns to the *permisso* he must fill out if we are to be allowed in.

Having taken step one, we feel we must go all the way, and to his questions about who we are and what we do we try to explain our new vocabulary: apostolate, mission, and poverty (about which he needs no explanation as all Mexico knows what poverty is). He is wary. He looks from side to side to see if colleagues or superiors are overhearing and leans closer as if to coach us — to say what's on his mind.

"When you do your mission you teach, si?"

"Well, yes, that's part of it, because we are an APOSTOLATE."

"No no no," he corrects; his long-lashed eyes hold our puzzled ones. "You are teachers." He encourages us like a first-grade teacher to repeat after him, "We are teachers." Click click. Paul and I exchange the sort of look we flash to each other on stage when one of us drops a line and the other is expected to fill the embarrassing pause. Aha! We are teachers! Being an apostolate on a mission is a worrisome thing in a country hostile to public religious instruction. (More worrisome, evidently, than being a married woman travelling with an unmarried man!) And bless his heart, this official representative of Mexico has saved us. "*Bueno*," he says. We've passed the test. We're in. *Olé*!

On a spotless Mexican bus we sit tall, hands clasped. Our crowded complement is escorted by an armed guard for the first hour — well! He gets out after expelling two characters who have more than a whiff of pot and who knows what else in their bulging suitcases.

There's no heater. We cover up with coats, sweaters and scarves until a bewildering dawn greets us. Not just any dawn, not a spectacular dawn, but a sky that pulls back its curtain revealing the first hint of distant mountains, dark, almost hidden, but there. The bus driver's sing-song announcement, Mon-te-ray, stops us in mid-yawn. Breakfast.

Lightness and brightness at this little bus stop crowded with hungry *campesinos* when an English-speaking elderly lady in leg braces, moving with a walker, warns us, "Don't be about in Mexico City after dark; that's where I was mugged and beaten."

So we arrive in Mexico City at nine p.m. and it is after dark.

A young man offers us a welcoming handshake, commends his taxi: "Clean. Safe. Prompt delivery."

Are we sure we want all this? He already has our luggage stowed away. Our only "want" is for him to get us — "deliver" if he chooses — to the Benedictines for safekeeping.

It is now nearing ten o'clock.

He scrutinizes the address we hand him. "*No problema. Bueno.* My name Hernandez."

Start! Jerk to a sudden halt in the middle — THE MIDDLE — of a traffic circle and a tough-looking hombre invites himself to join us, jumps into the front passenger seat, slams the door, and includes himself in our party. Loud greetings. Introductions.

"*Mi amigo*," our driver assures us, "Francisco. After work we dance."

Paul mumbles That's as good a cover story as I've heard, and with lots of Spanish between the driver and his friend, we're off again. Now the two of them begin to question the address. We begin to question their intentions. Terrified. My mental archives unreeling headlines: ploys, revolutionary stratagems — KIDNAP! We cruise street after street of suburbia's fortified residences encased in cement blocks for sly eyes to peer. O God! I plead to Paul sotto voce, Let's pray, point to the rosary dangling over the dashboard. We make the Sign of the Cross. A lone street lamp catches our reflection in the rear-view mirror and we see both men excitedly cross themselves. Hernandez takes his hands off the wheel to do it. Francisco's ringed fingers swiftly reprimand him with a swift swat to the head. "*Virgin Santissima de Guadalupe!*" Our *campaneros* who could be kidnappers interrupt each other with questions directed at us like ping-pong balls. We bat answers back in our own *lingua franca*. Where do we come from? What do we do? (Especially that one.) We say theatre artists and strike gold. *Teatro!* Password and passport to their Latin hearts. Like what? Like drama for example about San Francisco d' Assisi.

"*Divino Hijo*!" Francisco says; "*Hablo*, *hablo*, I am name after heem!"

Hernandez brakes, slaps the horn, and announces, *La Casa Benedictine!*

We stagger from the cab, our *amigos* bring our luggage to the unlighted door, and Hernandez refuses to accept payment. *Nada!* We exchange *abrazzos*. His friend shyly gives me a silver ring from his finger: "For you to pray for me, *this* Francisco." Fiat. I promise. The boys scramble back into the taxi with the same noisy slams that had terrified us an hour earlier. We call our *adios* to the disappearing taxi.

It is now nearing eleven o'clock.

I said before I love to tell the Jesus story, him and his glory, but actually I get as tired of it as Joseph and Mary must've become, plodding from place to place looking for space. Take for instance the two of us standing in front of a closed door sure of welcome. We had a letter of introduction from Father Kern, a man affectionately respected among the Mexicans as an exemplary priest. Every Lent he spends six weeks on pilgrimage here, immersing himself in their language and culture for the benefit of his own parishioners back home.

We knock. We wait. A man in civvies opens the door a slit. *Si?* We give him the letter, he scans it quickly, shrugs, says Follow me. We climb the stairs. He offers no help with our suitcases, but leads us to a small anteroom from which we glimpse some men playing cards to the sound of an American TV laugh track. A young priest comes through the archway fixing his dog collar, says Hi, rustles our letter at arm's length, shakes his head. Don't know anything about this; our Superior's out of town. I'll see what can be done. He exits fanning the letter as if putting out a match. The man who'd shown us in says You'd better sit down, it may be a while.

It's eleven-thirty.

Finally, an older priest stands in front of our nodding heads. "We can't put you up here. The Sisters of Cristo Rey will take care of you tonight."

Once more we are driven. A resentful Benedictine Brother catapults us in a Chevy through the poorest slums in town. It seems another ride that will never end when abruptly he turns and brakes in a bricked alleyway. Its exit is sealed by a metal wall. *Convento*, he announces, and pulls a bell rope that brings a nun's candlelit face to the huge iron gates.

It is midnight.

She carefully unlocks the gate bolt by bolt, smiles and softly says *Bienvenido* — our first welcome by a religious in Mexico City.

The unhappy chauffeur drops our luggage, reverses, and leaves faster than we can say thank you.

We follow the portress through a tunnel-like structure over cracked marble floors, up winding staircases heavy with quiet, to my room, large, windowless, unfurnished — just a bed and a chair. Then Paul is taken away. His footsteps recede in the ever-deepening night. I shiver at the grotesque shadows silhouetted on the wall by one dim light hanging above my bed. Giving up the fight against fatigue, I undress, burrow into my raincoat, curl under the cold covers, stretch out for the first time in three days.

And sleep.

Sueno ... to dream ...

* * * * *

In the castle the King, surrounded by sycophants and ambitious sophisticates, raises his hand in dismissal.

"Enough of sibilants," he says, and the court disperses. All but one man too drunk to find the exit. The King crooks his little finger and sings in a most melodious voice:

"*Vene*, you who are too full of the wrong spirits. I have a task for you."

The drunk makes an effort to fix his collar and straighten his scapular, but unable to walk in a straight line falls to his knees, answering in what purports to be harmony:

"*Credo*, Your Majesty."

"Yes, Rocco, that's why I selected you to be my Prime Minister," says the King.

"Prime Minister! But lordgod-almighty I can't even stand straight!"

"O you will. Once you do as I say."

The King whispers, "Just open your heart *all* the way. And promise not to close it until it's filled with every sin and sorrow of the whole world."

* * * * *

Awake from frozen sleep. Bells chime a call to riseRISErise. Early morning Mass at Cristo Rey Convent. We receive the Eucharist.

* * * * *

O my God! Where do dreams begin? Do they ever end?

* * * * *

There, at the altar, enveloped in white linen and surmounted by candles, he stands, the priest in my dream — or a refugee from Graham Greene's mixed bag of morose religious; I recognize him in the drinking of the wine. His prematurely aged face fills me with sadness and guilt.

* * * * *

The elegant, austere, and compassionate Mother Superior of Cristo Rey gently but firmly tells us that the rule is to offer hospitality for one week only. She leans toward us to suggest we establish contacts to provide for us while we focus our apostolate's mission: to discover Our Lady of Guadalupe. We're told that the Basilica of Guadalupe has a hostel for pilgrims. We go there.

The administrator was busy: so many altars in the shrine; so many priests guiding tour groups; so many Masses in so many languages. So much to be arranged. He had his lists. He put down his pen after checking a column or two, scanned our references quickly, and just as quickly informed us that there was no room, no hostel available. His eyes never met ours; never left his lists. *Adios* was never spoken.

We went into the Basilica to pray to The Lady.

We return to Cristo Rey and are called once more to Reverend Mother: "Rules," she smiles, "are made to be broken. You may stay as long as you need."

Did the Virgin send our apostolate back to Cristo Rey to taste simple poverty? Their convent, a once magnificent *casa*, is now cracked stone and blistering plaster. Here they honour the Benedictine rule that pilgrims are to be received as Christ himself.

The nuns pushed warming carts the length of a city block to bring hot food to us in the pilgrims' dining room. The building was unheated (and unheatable!) and this was one of the coldest Februaries on record. We ate wearing gloves, scarves, hats and coats. Our plates were served by hands too young to be red with chilblains, backs bent too soon with arthritis. Yet this was a joyous household. It was embarrassing: we were not to lift a dish, wash a cup, sweep a floor, only to eat and be satisfied. What they went without in order to provide us with pollo, tortillas, enchiladas, huevos, tea and coffee, breads and desserts, only God and the Guadalupe Lady knew. It was a poverty and a spirit of poverty simultaneously thrilling and humiliating. But the beauty of the convent was its location pointing to the Morning-Evening Star. There was a direct passage through a broken back door to Her and Her formidable old Basilica. Every day we went there to fulfill my mission from Father Kern to explore and discover Her whom I began to see as that Lovely Lady; to create something for the youth of his Mexican parish in Detroit's Corktown.

Wanting to stay close to those in the plaza gravitating to the Lady of Guadalupe on their knees; to those upright hurriedly approaching for a few fervent minutes during their demanding days; to those in military uniform staying only until Mass began, when post-revolutionary custom demands they leave; to those helpless such as myself bewilderedly hunched over an ungiving pew, pleading for direction:

In truth, what do I know about the Virgin, any virgin? Physically I don't qualify. But as an artist, a creative theatre-maker, I want my work unsullied, chaste. From the earliest frenzied days — harking back to my childhood friend Irene, and later my spiritual guide Fr. Rover — I'd attached myself to the rosary and asked Jesus' mother for help. No strings. I believed her authentic purity and a yearning began to grow in me, a yearning to stay close to her.

There was still another Mexican taxi ride to come. After a workshop at the Jesuit University we were given a "lettuce handshake" — a fistful of dollars.

"You've been working hard, living poorly, you need a rest. Here's the address of a pension in Acapulco. Our priests use it when they need to flake out." This was the Jesuit's witnessing of the Benedictine Rule toward pilgrims. They telephoned the woman who ran it to expect us.

We arrived in Acapulco late in the afternoon. Only one taxi left at the bus terminal. He had no meter. The tips-for-tourists brochure said, "Negotiate in advance." The middle-aged driver looked not unlike a New York cabbie of minor mafia connections. "*Si, si, si, no problema.*" But there was. The address the Jesuits had given us didn't exist; not the street, not the number. We began a circuit of the city. No help was to be found. The day waned. Paul became catatonic, I more and more nervous. ("*Senor*, we should know how much extra ... the cost ... " brought only "*Si, no problema.*") The driver stopped at his relatives' homes, then at the house where he knew the Anglican priests lived. Nothing. Sunset began to overshadow us. The driver was as tired by this time as we were frightened. He mumbled something about a *padre*, orphans, and again, *no problema*, and drove us out of town on a divided highway heading to the hills.

Now I was hysterical — partly about how much all this was going to cost — and Paul was furious with me for talking him into leaving home in the first place. The driver had given up trying to reassure us. I think he just wanted to dump us. He left the highway and bumped us over dirt roads, twisting and turning, and finally to a driveway where he braked to a halt, raising dust in a play-yard filled with children, lots of them. We got out of the taxi and I sat on a bench trembling and crying. The driver brought the priest in charge of this orphanage and left, glad to get away. Like Hernandez before him he accepted not a centavo for the trip.

The priest didn't know the address of the pension either.

"After the children are taken in to supper I'll make some phone calls. And don't worry," he said; "if worst comes to worst you can stay here overnight." He was very gruff when he said to Paul, "Tell her to stop crying!"

We were left alone in the yard, me sitting on that bench, Paul standing at the far end of it. I said we should pray to Our Lady of Guadalupe. Paul said what the hell has that ever brought us! He receded into silence; I fingered my rosary and prayed.

A loud low-slung Alfa Romeo sidled into the yard. I saw a lonely little boy's face staring at it through the dining-room window. From the far side of the car emerged a well-coiffed American blonde, and from the driver's seat a Latin Lothario with shirt open to the waist and a hairy chest boasting a huge crucifix. Well — judge not! We soon learned that she was the daughter of Darryl F. Zanuck, head of Twentieth Century Fox in Hollywood, who with her husband, the Lothario, spearheaded the international fundraising for this orphanage!

"Of course I know the woman and the pension you're looking for. Let me make a phone call." And then, "She's been wondering where you were!"

The city of Acapulco had a habit of changing street numbers and names without bothering to notify anyone. We'd been by the pension a half-dozen times in our frantic trips around the centre ring of the circus that had been this day's tour. We were driven directly to it in the loud and low-slung Alfa Romeo.

And there a woman stood at an open door, waiting. Exhausted, I came toward her, but she saw me stagger and reached out with both hands, folded me in a motherly *abrazzo*, and with soft pitying sounds led me to the nearest chair. Her black hair fell forward like a protective screen as she undid my sandals and cooled my swollen feet with wet white cloths. Ignoring the lateness of the hour and other guests passing through the hallway, she patted alcohol on my neck and forehead. Like a litany she murmured, "*Madre de Dio, Santissima de Guadalupe*," and gently kneaded the fear and anxiety from my poor body.

Ah!

Poverty appears in and assumes many guises, some sharper than any two-edged sword: unbelieving rejection, condescension, exclusion. I had come to Mexico to discover Our Lady of Guadalupe; I found her here. I had thought that my mission was to write a play about her and Juan Diego, the peasant she inveigled into gathering Castilian roses from barren rock, and that the purpose of my apostolate was to flesh out and make real the meaning, the significance, of the heroic struggles of holy/whole women and men who walk with Christ, embracing the witness of that demanding Lady of Guadalupe.

* * * * *

One day I saw a prostitute at the entrance to Our Lady's Basilica. I watched her leave her anxious client, make the Sign of the Cross, shuffle off her sandals and, head bowed, enter.

Was she cleaning up her act? Could she? Could I?

Scenes unreel:

> *I am at one and the same time seated in the dock and among the jury; I am the prosecutor and the defence attorney and, of course, the judge. Always THE JUDGE — who is not any god I know but myself. The defence attorney offers a supermarket special. Argument: childhood/adolescent little orgies smear youthful shamed faces — not sharp*

enough to claim headlines or footnotes in psychiatric textbooks — and he/she submits blame, lots of blame as excuse, explanation, rationale. Moves for acquittal.

In the dock, my chained hands beat my thighs Guilty, guilty, guilty, my pretty bony feet soundlessly scratch the floor spelling innocent until proven ordinary. Or not ordinary. What will be the verdict? Above the judge's head there is a crucifix. On it, Jesus' aged face carved by time, then mine, wrinkled, puzzled, and finally clear, crystal-cut — the Virgin or ... the Woman at the Well? Or Our Lady of Guadalupe?

Or Woman?

There she stands:

1970.
Having risen from my knees; alone in that studio in Palmer Rapids; having prayed, begged, cried out sobbing before the crucifix, TAKE THIS APPETITE FROM ME!

I have never written of this, referred to it rarely and then only in hope of helping someone. Afraid of false pride, I must rein in excessive emotion. I will try to allow the fact, the truth of that day, hour, time, *instant* when Christ took over and I have never since indulged, appeased, needed or wanted sexual fulfillment in any shape manner or form.

I had been convinced that, particularly for a woman and an artist, the sexual appetite, the drive for power was "natural." Prayer led me to cry out for celibacy, for absolute abstention, for a passion to see the meaning of authentic purity in myself and in my art.

There she stands, Our Lady.

I believe her.

* * * * *

"Fall on your knees ... " As in any withdrawal, my subconscious brought forth its dreams, yet there was no struggle, no temptation from that moment on. "Fall on your knees ... " Where does that hymn come from? It ran through my head all day yesterday, and I can hear it as I sit by this river now. My path was not the Ottawa River path I walk today; it was over the Canadian border with the Customs approval stamp and the weighing in of everything a U-haul could carry.

Today the river is drab, the clouds mottled. Stillness is settling over trees, water. I watch a motionless pigeon on the river's retaining wall, mouth agape for crumbs.

It's September now. The Ottawa River is swift. The traffic with its hustle is muted. I sit on the prickly grass, let its cropped beard scratch memory.

There's a special type of beetle that feeds on the foliage of roses; the dictionary says it has horny hard forewings that protect and cover its membraneous flight-wings. Now there's a metaphor: my hard persona masked the person that was emerging from my scripts to shake off my hardness and take winged flight with the Holy Spirit. It has been a bumpy flight, soaring then crash-landing.

I was a zealot, an impassioned missionary leader for a few years. Our Moving Word Centre apostolate changed homes, countries, toured Canada, the United States, Mexico, Italy. Christ knocked on my door and was welcomed. The significance of my journey seems a certainty.

* * * * *

Here for twenty hours I've been trying to get information about the name of the restaurant in Rome to which that Irish priest took me to dinner in 1976; as I remember it was called Living Waters or something similar ... hmmm ... phoned the Archdiocesan office, was transferred to an information person, spoke to a tape, left name, number, question. No reply yesterday or this morning. Repeated. Transferred again. This time great bewilderment, *non sequitur* suggestions ... Maybe someone at the Nunciature could help???, transferred AND WAITED — almost gave up. Suddenly in a flash I remembered St. Gabriel, Patron of Communications.

Gabriel patron of ALL communications ... Click!

– *Buon giorno*, hello, hello, this is Monsignor Alfredo, yes, yes, just here from Rome to help out for a month ... restaurant? yes, of course, you are right, *Living Waters*, a lay apostolate, offshoot of the Carmelites.

– WHAT!

– Yes yes you know St. Teresa of Avila?

– DO I KNOW? Are you kidding? Teresa of Avila and Thérèse of Lisieux raised the curtain and spotlighted my theatre form.

– That restaurant is on Chiara Square.

Click! *Chiara*! St. Claire of Assisi, Patron of Television. O how these little chicks come home to roost! O my Lord and my God, why do you treat me like a Jewish princess? Remember Thérèse of Lisieux: "Lord, don't treat me like an expensive toy. Fling me on the ground. Leave me neglected in a corner. Or — if it makes you happy, press me to your heart."

* * * * *

I muse by the Ottawa River, which has become my river.

Who are these women I once was and barely recognize as I riffle through candid and posed portraits and snapshots? This is Sara? A multiple personality? No psychiatrist ever thought so; best they arrived at was neurotic, imaginative — artist you know, very temperamental, a *little* unhinged ...

Well, let me tell *you*: out of her dreams, her un and subconscious ... out of the water in her mother's belly, pushed through living waters by ship to Algeria, plane to Morocco, the same to Italy, and Keystone-cabbed through Yugoslavia and Mexico, too, convoys colliding. Travelling land ... sea ... in the air ... catapulted ... somersaulted ... through terrifying space ... in and out of the States, sometimes to Sidney Bechet's sweet horn (he comforteth me on the steps of his cabin in the Borscht circuit) O! that long ago Depression summer so black and white; Bechet protected me from mockery at table in the presence of Manzie Johnson the drummer and the hungry jovial musicians when I asked what are sweetbreads? Bechet ever-so-gently took my hand and said testicles.

Now I dive with pointed toes, outstretched arms paddling, sinking, taking deep breaths and rising. I laugh, choke on new-found joy, turn over from the depths of this river — this source. Is this what's called eternity?

* * * * *

It's late afternoon. I rest my head on a tree's gnarled root, open my eyes, look up at the oak leaves' black undersides. The breeze picks up and with it the slender limbs shift, not quite dead, still pushing with autumnal resistance. Not yielding. Not yet.

AFTERWORD

IN MRS. STADELMAN'S WORK new forms manifest an age-old mythos. Like Wisdom, "she brings forth out of her treasure new things and old." The finest insights and inclinations of contemporary art are there, its passion for the simple and strong, for the pure line, for the lyric movement rising out of joy or wrenched out of pain, its nostalgic love of childhood, its anxiety, its sadness, its *demand* for God and the absolute. At its worst, contemporary art is submerged in matter and senses; it moves sluggishly or frenetically, appointed by chaos, driven or frozen by the madness of the infra-rational. At its best, it turns out like a battered sunflower toward the divine. In either case it cries out for God, for a Saviour. Roualt taught us this once and for all; Camus is trying to teach us, though his tongue sticks sometimes on those awkward affirmations; Dylan Thomas taught us by talent and tragedy as he fell back from his search for innocence, exhausted by passion, caught in a crossfire of contending loves. But all pointed to the same thing at last, that modern art is essentially a theological art, a religious art. Those who miss this point find themselves armed with great artistic weapons for the conquest — of nothingness!

I am guilty of provoking understatement when I say that my friend Mrs. Stadelman has not missed the point; she stands in very fact upon it as upon a moving point of rest in a dancer's flowing stride, so well equipped is she by training, temperament and vision for a conquest of the divine through the strong limbs of the choric art.

— Rev. Dominic Rover, O.P.

A Personal Appreciation

PAUL MACKAN

IN AN AGE OF CYNICS it is difficult to find a person committed to hope. It is also difficult if you do find one. In an era of liberation theories, a person committed to service rather than self is an anomaly indeed. In a society that stresses, with Eric Gill, that "every man [sic] is a special kind of artist," an artist can become superfluous.

Sara Lee (Harris) Stadelman is a small woman and a grand person. She is an artist whose hope has always been that her art would serve her church. I first met her forty years ago. Her work had just burst upon theatregoers and proved that our religious heritage could make exciting contemporary art for audiences of many faiths, or none.

Her theatrical experiments began at Immaculate Heart College in Los Angeles. She made a play of the Magnificat, using only the words of that prayer. It was performed as a dance-drama — a narrator reciting, dancers interpreting. Her second play, also a dance-drama, was *Teresa of Avila*, composed exclusively of direct quotations from the saint, and it brought her nationwide attention in the United States. She went on, having already completed her professional training in New York, to have a great impact upon the National Catholic Theater movement throughout the sixties.

Mostly there were new beginnings. That was partly because of audience response and partly because of the nature of the works themselves. Her audiences were familiar with the dance-drama form. But when she used it she brought to it her formidable talent as a choreographer — trained by Martha Graham no less. People responded as to something *new*. But Sara knew differently. She was dissatisfied with the form, even though it seemed there was no other available as a vehicle for her nascent artistic vision, sensing that the spectator was only being *told* about the drama (narrator) and only *watching* its interpretation (dancers). How could she get her audience *involved* in the heart of the matter?

As so often in her life, it was a saint who forced her to face the problem and find its solution. The saint was Thérèse of Lisieux. The problem? Stage = Action; Thérèse = Contemplative. To be resolved: How do you make an active person for the dramatic stage of a woman whose whole dramatic adventure with Christ was *interior*?

In 1959, at Catholic University in Washington, D.C., the curtain rose on The New Canticle. The audience rose to cheer. This was no longer dance-drama, for the narrator was missing. The dancers themselves were speaking — or the actors were dancing — doing both at once. The audience said, "This is a new form." For Sara it was a rediscovery of ancient forms. The critics cried, "the word *moves*." Sara later named it Choreologia, and it is still her Registered Trademark.

Despite this important breakthrough in the art of drama, "new beginnings" continued to be the hallmark of her maturing career as a Christian artist. Her extensive use of movement caused people to think of her as a dancer, while in fact she is an actor who happens to know dance and choreography thoroughly. In all her plays, the stylized dance movement is an organic extension of the acting. Playwright Emmett Lavery perceived the subtle difference when he said, "Sara Lee Stadelman is doing for the theatre what Martha Graham is doing for the dance."

For seasoned theatre and concert buffs there was no confusion. Sara's work was *theatre* and *art*. But even earlier attempts at religious dance by The Grail had not prepared Catholic audiences for the explosion of beauty and truth that she created. Gone were all the recognizable trappings of religious drama. When Sara's Teresa of Avila spoke of or to God, she did not automatically kneel with folded hands and raise her eyes heavenward. (Sara Lee was trained at The Neighborhood Playhouse, where Sanford Meisner banished any actor guilty of using such a cliché.)

The tradition of religious drama was, and unfortunately still is, literal romanticism. Sara's art is abstract, the form Thomas Merton called "the most natural locus for twentieth-century concern."

While audiences responded to the excitement of this new approach to religious art, some among them became uneasy with its implied criticism of traditional Catholic drama. To quote Thomas Merton again, "The protest of the abstract expressionist against conventional forms, subject matter and themes has been and remains a deeply spiritual protest. Spiritual at least implicitly, and in its intention. Quite contrary to the absurd cliché of the philistine who believes that abstract art is somehow faked, there is no kind of artistic creativity which depends more completely on sincerity, on the awareness of truth and falsity in one's motives, than abstract expressionism."

Sara had become, I think, the first abstract *theatre* artist in North America. She had achieved the kind of stylization on the stage that only later made Fellini famous in film. This is not generally recognized because she did the better part of her work in sectarian circles. She wanted with all her heart to place her talent at the church's service. However, she found herself at sea. She was the mainstream, but was running against the current.

When she was a young actress on Broadway, never out of work, one critic said of her, "She has the comedy timing and delicatesse of Chaplin." One of her closest advisors told her she had "New York at her feet." She confounded that world by giving it up, and then confounded the church world even more by taking it up.

In the church milieu, where one could understandably expect to see a spirit of conviction, Sara found a degree of confusion — also understandable. Church people had at that time no contemporary experience of artists with a capital "A." The church's traditional role as patron of the arts, while a source of justifiable pride, had been dropped as a current activity. Her pride was in her past.

When I was growing up, the church's experience of the arts was the same as that of society at large. Piano, ballet (for *girls*), and drama were generally leisure activities used to no other purpose than to teach social grace and an acceptable degree of confidence in self-expression. Sculpture was statuary. Period. Church choirs and parish events usually reflected this attitude, and our parish schools certainly did not expose us to the imaginations of great artists, who, if they were not already on "the list," might well be by the end of term. In short, I got the impression that the arts were only too uncertain, certainly unsettling, and that artists were "bohemian." Shakespeare, of course, was taught and quoted (after editing), but no sincere effort was made to find and nurture a successor.

A certain stable plateau had been reached, and resting upon it looking to the laurels of the past seemed the best thing for society as a whole. The church was preoccupied with carving a place for herself in that society, and securing her own stability. A laudable and necessary work, but it meant that artistic endeavours were undertaken within the parish and were therefore limited in financial and creative scope. What then to do with an artist to whose work people were responding enthusiastically even though they were thought not to be "ready for it"?

Sara could not help but contribute to the confusion, because her work took religious celebration once again to the level of art and catapulted it into the arena of public concern. With the general public came the professional critics. Without contemporary precedents the consternation of the church was easy to appreciate.

The critics watched figures such as Mary, Teresa, or Magdalene presented on Sara's stage, and wrote and spoke not of interesting sectarian themes, but of "theatrical magic," and "the most effective and dramatic presentations of the season." Subsequently one of them demanded, on radio, "Why are the sisters hiding this first-rate artist behind that forbidding iron fence?" (They were not, of course.) This definitely didn't help the situation.

In fact, there was no "situation," but simply the coming together of two quantities unknown to each other: Sara wanting to serve and celebrate her church; the church unwilling to trust, and with reason. The church and the artist had for generations lived in an uneasy separation —divorce not being allowed.

As there were within the church those already long-prefiguring Vatican II, so there were and are those fine men and women, religious and laity, whose spiritual truth allows and makes it possible for the Holy Spirit to demolish the oft-laid plans of mice and others. They found ways to nurture and encourage Sara.

She grew in her work and with that opened the doors for the crowds of liturgical dancers, actors, and entrepreneurs to tumble through. She continued to mature and refine her concepts, struggling always to achieve greater art. Today, almost totally unacknowledged by those whose path she cleared, she stands still one giant step ahead of them. Choreologia™ is not interpretive, not representational, but incarnational. It goes beyond the intermittently charming romanticism of Godspell to present *Truth-Alive-and-Well-and-Living-in-Us*.

In 1968-69 Sara moved to Canada, became a citizen, and founded The Moving Word Centre (Choreologia™: "the word moves") as an apostolate for artists of all genres, "to assist the church in realizing the value of employing the arts and artists *professionally* in communicating the message and witness of its faith."

She believes in both the necessity and possibility of a reconciliation of the church and the artist, and as a step toward achieving it, has radically revised her own way of life. She lives with religious promises, prays, creates, and tries to welcome those who want consultation, rest, or work.

Others more capable and less involved than I will have to speak of the theology or ecclesiology of The Moving Word Centre and its philosophical or social ramifications. Sara's commitment has been to the training and maturing of artists, and to her conviction that religious art must be *art*.

At present the Canadian church still tosses the arts into a general grab-bag, so Sara's goal of a nationwide apostolate (ministry) of artists — if not under one roof, then perhaps forming a malleable network — supported in simple dignity and given a mandate by the church to celebrate the faith with poetry, literature, drama, dance, sculpture, architecture, and music is yet to be realized.

Still, Sara has produced some of the most memorable moments in modern drama, religious or secular: the wit and humour with which a blue-clad, red-haired Virgin of Guadaloupe inveigled Juan Diego in *Touch the Mountain* (1968); the jazz improvisation on the Canticle of the Sun when Francis and Clare of Assisi met in the fiery scene from *Chiara* (1963); Thérèse of Lisieux springing gamin-like to the edge of the stage to tell the audience, "I am going to be a saint," in *The New Canticle* (1959); the great famine scene from *Western Testament* (1965); the dramatization of human love, of which there are few equals in theatre history, that Sara realized between Jocasta and Oedipus in her *The Passion of Jocasta* (1967), in which she dared to interlace this great Greek drama with the Passion of Good Friday to create a profoundly prophetic celebration of woman; the chilling clarity of the moment when individual conscience and choice swept away the theologies and philosophies surrounding abortion in *The Eve of Genesis* (1971). (It was in her 1974 play, *The Memoirs of a Master-Builder*, that she coined the phrase "abortion *after* birth," and it has remained part of the current theme.)

Sara Lee is also registered with the British Museum and the New York Public Library as the first person in theatre history to stage Shakespeare's sonnets as a play — its complete dialogue being *only* the sonnets. *The Detroit Free Press* said of *The Dark Lady Within*, "Sara Lee Stadelman makes Albee look like a sissy and Ionesco tongue-tied."

The argument most frequently put forward by the church (and by the society it wants to be part of) is that the artist should find a job, like any ordinary person, and not make financial demands upon the church. (Wilfrid Sheed tackled this problem very nicely in *The Hack*.) Sara writes of how ill she has made herself trying to be ordinary. This suffering is sometimes misread as "artistic temperament," but it isn't. Rather, it's a vulnerability to openness and caring that is common to artists and is the source of their creative strength.

She denies any claim to scholarship, yet no written work or play of hers has ever been faulted theologically. She does admit, however, to a "formidable power of observation and a prophetic instinct." Her mature experience can discern the difference between the communication desired and the reality achieved. And it is not to earn economic comfort that she demands from the church just hire for her professional labours. She cares to the point of hurting that the church's prevailing ignorance of the arts and the artist's role means that the church lacks the nourishment of one of the Spirit's most exciting manifestations.

She is Martha. And as Martha was told to "cool it," so Sara has been tempered by friends and supporters with the need for patience and perseverance. And an ambivalence in Sara herself has made it difficult for some church people to respond to her goal. She has striven with determination for recognition of her work, and with determination she has run from success, distrusting "too much identity," and with it loss of independence from the pulls of factions. She withdrew from the networks of workshops and seminars and conferences where the factions' pulls are exercised. She will not be anyone's guru. Nor will she follow those who would be. What is often perceived, then, is a person who energetically denies being special, but who demands the acceptance of her special contribution.

The dichotomy has not served her well. New generations have come who don't know of her, and can't acknowledge her contribution. In 1997 Pope John-Paul II elevated Thérèse of Lisieux to the rank of Doctor of the Church. In the celebrations Sara's groundbreaking *The New Canticle* was not recalled or re-staged. The fashion, as it were, has changed. The social sciences have brought us to believe in the equality of all creative efforts and the arrogant divisiveness of criticism. Sara, on the other hand, while kindly disposed toward and convinced of the healing power of the arts in the lives of the wounded—which includes all of us—insists upon standards: "It may be therapy, but please don't call it poetry," or music, or dance, unless it meets art's criteria as well. And she is nowhere more critical than with her own work.

So it is, in that sense, as if her work is of the past while she is intensely present, writing, envisioning, living the spiritual promises she made and witnessing to her church's still unrecognized and unfed need. She also sets aside any insistence by anyone that to be a Christian artist is to be in some way limited in scope.

Her goal of a ministry of and for artists has not yet come about, but her vision remains eminently worthwhile. In the early 1980s, John W. Cook, associate professor of religion and the arts at Yale University, wrote, "Contemporary influences have theology riding off in all directions at once, and the resulting impression is that things are at a standstill. I suggest that on the horizon is an integrative force for theology and ministry, that when taken seriously, significantly influences and shapes theological education, Christian ministry and worship. The integrative force that will play an increasingly significant role ... is in the arts."

Sara is a master of the arts. And her eye is always on the horizon.

PHOTO CAPTIONS AND CREDITS

Jesus in the Window, Saralee Harris age 5, Atlantic City Boardwalk. Family photo.

Isa, Saralee Harris, Erasmus Hall High School, 1934. Moving Word Centre archives.

Martha, Sara Lee Harris. Malibu, California, circa 1946. M.W.C. archives.

Pursue Your Verb!, Broadway debut in Irwin Shaw's Sons and Soldiers, 1944. From L.: unidentified, Karl Malden, Gregory Peck, Sara Lee Harris. Photo: Fred Fehl.

Walk-Ons and Bit-Parts, At rehearsal. M.W.C. archives.

Intermission with 5 Minutes to Spare, Italy, 1944. ACME Photo.

The Strip, Bird Cage Theatre, Las Vegas, 1950. From L: Cate; Sara Lee Stadelman, Kris, Richard Ryerson Stadelman. M.W.C. archives.

One Encore After Another, Sara Lee Harris, Washington Square, circa 1938. Family photo.

Deepwood, Sara Lee Stadelman 1960. M.W.C. archives.

F.L.W., Frank Lloyd and Mrs. Wright, Taliesen East, 1956. Family photo.

Once More From the Top Entr'acte, "Teresa of Avila," Immaculate Heart College, Hollywood, California, 1957. M.W.C. archives.

Direct and Alternating Currents, Rehearsal for "The New Canticle," Catholic University of America, Washington D.C., 1959. M.W.C. Archives.

Ariadne Sleeps/Artemis Splits, Richard Stadelman, Athens, 1958. M.W.C. archives.

Gladys and Harold, Glad rehearsing "The Dark Lady Within." M.W.C. archives.

Split, Sara Lee Stadelman, circa 1965. M.W.C. archives.

There She Stands, Sara Lee Stadelman as Catherine Benincasa in the film, Catherine's Song, 1975. M.W.C. archives.

Back Cover, Sara Lee Stadelman, 1999. M.W.C. archives.